Growing In Christ

A HANDBOOK FOR ALL CHRISTIANS

Growing In Christ

GENE ROGERS

COLLEGE PRESS
PUBLISHING COMPANY
Joplin, Missouri

2nd Printing 1998

Library of Congress Catalog Card Number 94-72128
International Standard Book Number 0-89900-682-5

Contents

Acknowledgments

This book is a product of the ministry of the Normandie Avenue Christian Church of Gardena, California whose members gave me the time to write and encouraged me along the way.

I am particularly grateful to my wife Alice for all her encouragement and suggestions, to Lydia and Annette Annett who worked with me tirelessly typing and re-typing the many drafts and changes the manuscript underwent, to my daughter Beth for her technical assistance, to Rachel Setzer for proofing the final drafts, and to Loran Biggs, Dr. Gary Tiffin, Dr. Myron Taylor and Roger Beard who took time from their busy schedules to read and critique the rough draft and make valuable suggestions for its improvement.

Preface

I was a very excited young Christian following my decision to surrender to Christ as Lord. I had become a Christian as the result of a comprehensive reading of the four Gospels. God had immediately led me to become associated with a local congregation of believers. It was wonderful to be in company with people who had made the same life commitment that I had. I hoped to receive from those older and more mature Christians the teaching and nurturing that I knew I would need to enable me to mature in my newfound faith. I was warmly received into the fellowship of the church and integrated into its life. I was even given a junior boys' Sunday School class to teach. But as a baby Christian I wasn't given anything to help develop and mature me in Christ. There weren't any classes for new believers, no new member material, no shepherding plan, nothing like that. It seemed that somehow newborn babes were supposed to arrive at maturity on their own.

My growing up in the faith was something like that of a child growing up without the loving, nurturing care of parents. I was a "latch key" convert. I drug myself up. And it was a long, slow process with many failures along the way. I think I will always be somewhat spiritually retarded because I didn't receive the help I needed during my spiritual youth. I am confident that I would be much more mature and be much better equipped to serve Christ now if I had been nurtured when I first became a believer.

Since it took me so long to arrive at any kind of maturity in Christ, I have a special concern for the needs of those who are just starting out as Christians. I am keenly aware of their vulnerability. I know of the dangers that lurk before them. I know how limited their spiritual lives will be if they are not nurtured in their infancy, and cared for in their youth. I know that God's goal for them is maturity with all the added spiritual blessing that goes with it. And I long to see them grow up in Christ. To do this I know they will need help, and I want to make some kind of contribution.

From the day I first read of Paul's commitment to unceasing labor in counseling, teaching, and wisdom to bring every believer to maturity in Christ (Col. 1:28, 29), I have been inspired to do likewise. New believers have had a special place in my heart for a long time and I have done all that I know to do to help them grow as quickly as possible to maturity in Christ. Some of the things that I have shared with people which have served to help them grow I have put into writing and now offer with the hope that they may serve to help more young believers mature in Christ.

Whether you are a new Christian or the product of a congregation that didn't nurture you in the faith following your decision for Christ, what follows in this book is offered with the earnest prayer that it will help you to arrive at some degree of maturity in Christ.

1 Testing For New Birth

So you've become a Christian? You've been "born again" or "born of God." And maybe you thought your life was going to be instantly turned around. You anticipated that becoming a Christian would result in you immediately experiencing an altogether new and different life. Hadn't you been told by Christians that the Bible says, "if anyone is in Christ, he is a new creation; the old has gone, the new has come!" But so far you haven't been experiencing too much of the new. Oh yes, there was excitement and satisfaction when you made your decision for Christ. You may even have had the sense that a great weight was lifted off you and you may have felt clean and new at that time. But now that you have moved beyond the excitement of decision to the daily practicality of living as a Christian, you are finding that there is so much of the "old" still in your life that you are beginning to question if your decision was valid; you may wonder whether or not you were born of God in the first place. And certainly the enemies of your faith are doing all they can to convince you that you weren't.

CAN I KNOW IF I'VE BEEN BORN ANEW?

Maybe you've begun to think, "I sure wish there was some way that I could know for sure whether or not I've been born again. If only God had some kind of checklist I could go over to determine whether or not I have. Then I'd know. I could either pursue the new birth if I haven't, or get on with my Christian life if I have."

Well, God has such a checklist. And it is found in the little New Testament letter of 1 John. In this letter the Apostle John expresses great concern over whether believers have been born of God. So much so that he offers six identifying marks of the person who has been born of God so that everyone can make a determination.

CLARIFYING THE TEXT

In saying that there are six great marks of one "born again" or "born of God," we must recognize that there may be a vast difference in the depth and distinctness of these marks in different people. In some, the marks may be faint, tame, feeble, and hardly able to be discerned. While in others, they may be so bold, sharp, clear, and plain as to be easily read by anyone. And some of these marks will be more visible in some, while other marks will be more visible in others. It seldom happens that they are all equally manifested in one and the same person. But, nevertheless, the six marks will, in some degree, be evidenced in the life of everyone born of God.

Now then, what are the six marks?

BELIEVING IN CHRIST

First of all, John says, "Everyone who believes that Jesus is the Christ is a child of God, and everyone who loves the parent loves his child" (1 John 5:1). He who is born of God has committed his life in trust to Jesus Christ as his only Savior, and he loves Him. He has come to see clearly his awful predicament in sin and has accepted Jesus as his only means of deliverance. He may still have fears and doubts from time to time; at times he may even feel that he has no faith at all. But ask him if he is willing to trust anything or anyone except Christ for forgiveness and new life, and see what he'll say. Ask him if he will rest his hope of eternal life upon his own goodness, good works, prayers, church, or minister, and see what he'll reply.

Have you committed your life in trust to Jesus as your Savior?

PRACTICING RIGHTEOUSNESS

Secondly, John says, "You may be sure that every one who does right is born of him" (1 John 2:29). He who is born of God has begun to do what God's Word has shown him to be right. Whereas God had no control over his former life, he now endeavors to do God's will as it is revealed to him. His life is now one of continually looking to Christ as his life-controlling example as well as his Savior. He is far from being perfect; he fights a daily battle with sin; he stumbles often, but he'll usually say with John Newton, "I'm not what I ought to be, I'm not what I want to be, I'm not what I hope to be, but still I'm not what I used to be, and by the grace of God, I am what I am."

Have you begun to do what is right as God has revealed it to you?

LOVING OTHER CHRISTIANS

Thirdly, John says, "We know that we have passed out of death into life, because we love the brethren. He who does not love remains in death" (1 John 3:14).

He who is born of God has begun to be gripped by love for God's people. Like his Savior, he has love and concern for all men, but he has a special love for those who have come to have one mind with him about Jesus.

He is never so much at home as when he is with Christians–in their company. They are his family! And he longs to be with them. They are fellow soldiers with him warring against the same enemy. They are fellow travelers journeying with him on the same road toward the same destiny. He understands them, and they understand him. And though they may be very different in many ways–in rank, station, wealth, education–the important thing is, they are his brothers and sisters. They have the same loving Father and share the same life. He cannot help loving them.

Have you begun to be gripped by a love for the people of God?

NO HABITUAL SINNING

Fourthly, John says, "No one who is born of God makes a practice of sinning, because the God-given life-principle continues to live in him, and he cannot practice sinning, because he is born of God." (The Charles Williams translation of the New Testament).

He who is born of God has begun to stop rebelling against God and His will for his life. Before coming to Christ his life in general was characterized as being lived in rebellion against the will of God. Living life without God was the practice of his life and giving God a say so was the exception. Now that he has come to Christ, he has made "doing God's will" the practice of his life and rebellion against it has become the exception. He used to feel no grief over doing evil. He had no quarrel with sin; he and sin were friends. Now he hates sin, flees from it, fights against it, considers it a damnable plague, and longs to be evermore completely delivered from it.

This is not to say that he never sins any more. If he claimed this, he would be deceiving himself, there would be no truth in him, and he would be making God a liar (1 John 1:8, 10). He cannot prevent bad thoughts from arising within him, or shortcomings, omissions, and defects from appearing both in his words and actions. But you will hear him saying that these things are a daily grief and sorrow to him and that he longs for the day when they will be no more.

Have you begun to quit rebelling against God and his will for *your* life?

OVERCOMING THE WORLD

Fifthly, John says, "Whatever is born of God overcomes the world; and this is the victory that overcomes the world, our faith" (1 John 5:4).

He who is born of God has begun to experience a freedom from being dominated by the unbelieving people about him. He is no longer conforming to the world's standard and rule for life. He has quit living to please men. He doesn't mind going against the stream of the world's ways, notions, and customs. He is no longer trying to keep up with the Joneses. He is no longer concerned about "what will men say?" He now finds little pleasure in doing most of what the world around him is doing in its pursuit of happiness. He is now living to please God rather than men, and is more concerned about offending God than men. His first aim is to please God.

Have you begun to experience a freedom from being dominated by the unbelieving world of people around you?

KEPT FROM THE EVIL ONE

Lastly, John says, "We know that no one who is born of God makes a practice of sinning, but the Son who was born of God continues to keep him, and the evil one cannot touch him" (1 John 5:18, Williams translation of the New Testament).

He who is born of God has begun to experience that Christ steers him away from the temptations of the evil one so that he is less prone to being dominated by sin. The Christ who is within him has begun to strengthen and counsel him in the truth so that the temptations presented to him by the evil one are beginning to become less appealing and he finds himself surrendering to them less frequently. He has begun to surrender to the leading of the Spirit and has, therefore, become less vulnerable to Satan's appeals. He is finding as John said, "He who is in you is greater than he who is in the world" (4:4). That is, the Christ within him is greater in power and influence in him and upon him than is the devil.

Have you begun to experience that Christ steers you away from the temptation of the evil one so that you are becoming less prone to being dominated by sin?

HOW DID YOU DO?

Such are the six scriptural marks of being born anew. We can use them to test ourselves and to understand others who claim to have been born again. How did you do? Did you pass the test? Only those persons who are born again will have these six marks upon them. Those who do not have them are not born anew.

God wants us to be sure that we have eternal life. In 1 John 5:13 he has spoken to us through John saying, "I write this to you who believe in the name of the Son of God, that you may know that you have eternal life."

2 On to Maturity

Once you have accepted Christ as your Lord and Savior and have become a partaker of the life of God, your next concern should be to see that new life develops within you so that you can begin to be conformed to the image and likeness of Jesus.

Your new birth has brought you a new nature and with it all the potential of a blessed new life in Christ. But birth alone does not insure sustained life nor will it bring one into fullness of life in either the spiritual or physical realm. The fact that a baby is introduced to life in this world does not insure that it will live to experience adulthood. There are certain conditions that must be met to develop the life begun in it. If those conditions are met, the newborn will most naturally grow. But if they are not met, life will be extinguished almost as quickly as it began. If the basic necessities for the sustaining and developing of spiritual life are met, the new inward life begun can do nothing but grow. But if they are not met, spiritual life can be extinguished almost as quickly as it began.

BORN FOR MATURITY

Birth is a start in life – not the goal. The new birth is a start in the spiritual life; it is not the goal. When a baby is born it is not born to remain a baby during all its earthly life. The goal set before it at birth is adulthood and maturity. All of the nurture and care and discipline that the home gives, added to that which the school, public or private, has to contribute, plus all the experience that life itself offers, combine to bring the baby through the various growth stages to physical, mental, and emotional maturity. Maturity is the goal.

God does not lead us through the experience of the new birth and place his life within us for us to remain a spiritual baby. The new birth is only the beginning. God's will for each of us is that we grow to spiritual maturity. This is the goal that he has set for each one of us. All spiritual nurturing, every spiritual experience, every bit of spiritual discipline, and all Christian education combine to work for realizing that goal within us. God's desire is that every newborn babe be brought to maturity in Christ; he repeatedly says so in his Word. Consider some major passages in which his will is revealed on this matter. "Speaking the truth in love, we are to *grow up* in every way into Him who is the Head, into Christ" (Eph. 4:15, RSV, emphasis added). "Him we proclaim, warning every man and teaching every man in all wisdom, that we may present every man *mature* in Christ" (Col. 1:28, RSV, emphasis added). "As therefore you received Christ Jesus the Lord, so live in Him, rooted and *built up* in Him and established in the faith, just as you were taught, abounding in thanksgiving" (Col. 2:6, 7, RSV, emphasis added). "Therefore let us leave the elementary doctrines of Christ and go on to *maturity*" (Heb. 6:1, RSV, emphasis added). "But *grow* in the grace and knowledge of our Lord and Savior Jesus Christ" (2 Pet. 3:18, RSV, emphasis added). It is equally true in both the physical and spiritual realms that everything and everyone must either continually grow or die.

THE BLESSEDNESS OF MATURITY

A newborn baby in the home certainly has some capacity for experiencing satisfaction in being alive. It experiences satisfaction in nursing, in being held and cuddled, and in being talked to and made over by its parents and older members of the family. In a sense, we could say that these experiences are representative of the joy a baby is capable of knowing in its new found life, limited though these may be.

Contrast the baby's limited ability to experience joy in life with that of an adult. Contrast the baby's limited experience of nursing and being cuddled with the wide variety of experiences that adults are capable of entering into. Consider, for example, your own ability as an adult, to experience a wonderful evening dining at your favorite restaurant; consider the experience of spending an evening listening to your favorite orchestra; think of being able to experience the many joys of domestic relationships; or consider the excitement you could have while participating in your favorite sport. As you can see, the ability to receive of the blessings of this life is directly proportionate to the degree of your maturity. The greater our maturity the greater our capacity to receive and experience increasingly more of all that life has to offer in this world. An adult's capacity for experiencing life is hardly to be compared with that of a baby.

Similarly, there is certainly joy to be experienced by a newborn babe in Christ. To begin with, there is the joy resulting from being set free from the plaguing guilt of sin. There is joy in knowing that we have come into right relationship with God. And, there is joy in knowing that we have been freed from the fear of death, judgment and condemnation. But these blessings which come to us as newborn babes in Christ are not to be compared with those that can be ours as mature, adult believers in Christ. For though to be in Christ even as a babe certainly is a blessing in itself, it definitely has its limitations. The babe in Christ by the very fact of infancy is limited in ability to receive yet greater blessings that come with maturity in Christ. While yet a babe he must partake of the "pure spiritual milk" of the Word before he is able to partake of the "meat." (See 1 Peter 2:2, Heb. 5:12-14.) As a babe he is limited in his ability to experience many of the joys that are to be had in serving, because as a new convert he is not yet able to assume positions of responsibility and leadership out of which come many of the greater blessings of the Christian life (1 Tim. 3:6). The blessings that God is able to pour into our lives are directly proportionate to our degree of maturity and our ability to receive. With growth in Christ comes a greater ability to receive and experience increasingly more of God and the life that he has imparted to us.

Maturity in Christ should immediately become the desired goal of everyone born into the family of God. The new Christian should certainly be thrilled in being born into the family of God, but should immediately begin to earnestly long to quickly grow out of infancy where life is filled with unresolved questions and problems, where we are inexperienced in so many ways, and where we are lacking in mature knowledge, wisdom, and understanding. Increased happiness awaits us as we begin to move toward maturity in Christ, and fullness of life shall be ours when we finally arrive.

FOUR ESSENTIALS TO GROWTH

The basic necessities required to sustain the life of a baby seem to be four in number: nourishment, nurture, breathing, and exercise. Withdraw any one of these and a baby will not only fail to grow; it will die.

These same basic necessities must be met in the spiritual life if it is to be sustained and developed. The newborn babe in Christ must be nourished and nurtured and must breathe and exercise if the spiritual life begun within it is not to be extinguished. Let us devote some time to a consideration of these four basic essentials.

THE NEED FOR NOURISHMENT

It is quite obvious that the first basic need of a baby is food. If ever a baby is to grow to adulthood it certainly must be nourished. If all food were withdrawn from a baby it would be but a matter of time until it starved.

The newborn babe in Christ must be nourished or it will die. Spiritual birth must be followed by a systematic and regular feeding upon Christ (John 6:52-63). We may feed upon Christ by taking him into our lives through the Word of God. The Word of God reveals to us all that we may know of Christ and the life that He would develop within us. The Word of God is that spiritual food which must be consumed if we are to be nourished and have a developed life. Jesus said that "man shall not live by bread alone, but by every word that proceeds from the mouth of God" (Matt. 4:4).

If an infant is ever to grow to adulthood, and in so doing enjoy good health along the way, it must partake of nourishment daily. To fail to do so would result in weakness, sickness, and eventual death. Likewise, the new babe in Christ must partake of the Word of God by disciplined daily reading and study or he will become spiritually weak and sick and end up dying spiritually.

As a baby is fed and begins to grow, the need for nourishment in other areas begins to arise. We begin to give attention to fulfilling not only the physical but the mental and emotional needs that the child has. These needs may be met by the home until they are of high school or college age, or help may be sought from others in either private or public school. Whatever the case, there comes a time when the help of teaching specialists will be needed to further accelerate the growth of our children. They are going to need outside help when it comes time for them to enter into higher education.

The new Christian not only has a need for regular daily nourishment from a home study of the Word of God, but he also needs to be regularly confronted by specialists in the Word who will be able to aid him in reaching maturity much more quickly. There is not only the need for studying the Word of God daily personally, but there is also the need for assembling with the church where those who have been blessed with the gift of teaching (Eph. 4:10-16) can serve to accelerate growth by giving insight into the depth of the meaning of God's Word. While daily home study is mandatory for spiritual growth, it is of equal importance that we assemble with other Christians where the Word of God is expounded by more mature believers who serve as teaching specialists.

THE NEED FOR NURTURING

A second basic need of a baby is that of nurturing. A baby must be looked after, cared for, loved and handled if it is to reach adulthood. Research has proven that a baby left entirely to itself, though well fed, will nevertheless die. It must have contact with other human beings if life is to be sustained and developed within it.

If the spiritual babe is to grow to maturity in Christ it too must have nurture and care. It must be in constant contact with the older members of the family of God who have been commissioned by the Lord to look after the lambs. The new Christian cannot fend for himself anymore than a baby can take care of itself. He must have the encouragement and fellowship of the family of God. To fail to be actively associated with the family of God is to court spiritual disaster.

The new Christian needs to immediately assume his position as part of the church. He needs to regularly assemble with God's family for worship and study. He needs to take advantage of every opportunity for fellowship and seek the association of older believers who will be able to contribute to his spiritual growth.

Surely, if the fellowship of the church was not vital to the Christians' growth and maturity, the Lord would never have instituted such a fellowship in the first place and would not have devoted so much of Scripture emphasizing its importance, function, and value.

THE NEED FOR BREATHING

If a baby is to live to become an adult, the first breath taken at birth must be followed by a life of breathing. Breathing is vital to the sustaining of life. One must take into his body those elements of the atmosphere which are necessary to sustain life.

If the newborn babe in Christ is to stay alive spiritually and grow to maturity he must immediately begin, and maintain, a life of prayer. Prayer is the breath of the soul. It is through prayer that we are able to open our lives to more of God. Prayer is a means of vital contact with God. It is a way of fellowshipping with him and of discerning his will for our lives. It is a means of direct and immediate communication with our Father.

The new convert needs to develop and maintain a life of prayer even as a baby needs to take that first breath and continue breathing.

Jesus' example teaches us to pray (Matt. 14:23; Mark 1:35). Jesus told us to pray (Luke 18:1). The results of prayer demand that we pray (Matt. 7:7, 8; Phil. 4:5-7). To maintain or restore lost fellowship with the Father necessitates our praying (Matt. 6:6; 1 John 1:9; 2 Chron. 7:14). As new Christians our first request of the Lord should be "Lord, teach us to pray" (Luke 11:1).

THE NEED FOR EXERCISE

If a baby is ever to grow to adulthood it is essential that it exercise. It must exercise its mind and its limbs. To fail to do so is to run the risk of losing their use. For example, if one failed to use his right arm, he would lose the use of it. Exercise is a vital factor in growing from infancy to adulthood.

Those who become Christians must exercise their faith by serving God if they are to grow and reach maturity in Christ. The Christian life is characterized as a life of service.

In 2 Corinthians 5:15 we are told that to be a Christian is to live for Christ: "And he died for all, that those who live might *live no longer for themselves but for Him* who for their sake died and was raised" (emphasis added). In 1 Thessalonians 1:9 the Thessalonians were told that their conversion was one that had turned them "to God from idols, to *serve* a living and true God" (emphasis added). Jesus said that proof of our discipleship would be a fruit-bearing life: "By this my Father is glorified, that you *bear much fruit*, and so prove to be my disciples" (John 15:8, emphasis added).

God has given each of us talent, ability, and gifts of his grace to be employed in his service. It is his intention that we use them. "Having gifts that differ according to the grace given us, let us use them: if prophecy, in proportion to our faith; if service, in our serving; he who teaches, in his teaching; he who exhorts in his exhortation; he who contributes, in liberality; he who gives aid, with zeal; he who does acts of mercy, with cheerfulness" (Rom. 12:6-8). It is as we use these talents in Christian service that growth takes place, to say nothing of the fact that the work of the Lord is done through the service we render. If we do not exercise our faith in service it is quite easy to see that our growth will be seriously limited. We will probably never grow much beyond spiritual babyhood. It is essential to our growth, then, that we get vitally involved in Christian service.

INTERRELATIONSHIP OF NEEDS

Experience is going to teach you that these four basic growth needs are intricately interrelated. Their fulfillment does not take place as isolated experiences. Having one need met will naturally lead to the fulfilling of others. For example, to read and study God's Word and learn of the greater blessings He has in store for you as a believer will move you to lift up prayers of praise and thanksgiving. As you begin to search his Word you will be challenged and directed to Christian activity, and will become involved in Christian service before you hardly know it. As you read and study the Word, begin a life of prayer and start to serve, you will experience that you will not only want to do these things alone, but also along with other believers. You will come to see that studying the Word and praying with other believers will bring added spiritual blessings to your life. You will learn that the most effective way in which service can be rendered is in cooperation with fellow believers. Therefore, of necessity, you will find yourself sharing much of life with them in study, prayer, worship, and service.

In running a parallel between physical and spiritual growth, as we have been doing in this study, there is a great difference to be noted between the length of time required by each to reach maturity. Physical maturity is a lengthy process. One does not expect a baby to arrive at adulthood in less than 18 or 20 years, or even longer. Spiritual maturity may not require as much time. Spiritual maturity can be reached in a relatively short period of time if vigorously pursued. How quickly it is reached will depend upon how earnestly one yearns for it.

How fast can you grow? That depends entirely upon you. God grant that the desire of your heart will be to "grow daily in the grace and knowledge of our Lord and Savior Jesus Christ" and "to grow up in every way into Him who is the Head, into Christ," that you may be "mature in Christ."

3 Learning to Pray

One of the blessings of becoming a Christian is that you can talk to God with the assurance that he hears you and will answer you. Prior to your becoming a Christian you didn't have that assurance; maybe he would hear you and maybe he wouldn't. But now you can have an audience with him any time of day or night because you have become one of his children and he has extended that privilege to you.

Being able to speak to God at any time enables us to bring our weaknesses and needs to a caring, loving Parent that can supply and help. It also enables us to have a growing relationship with him. And having entered into the family of God we will certainly want to know our Father in the most intimate way possible.

But talking to God may be a completely new experience. You may never have done it before and you may not know how to go about it. You may need help in establishing it as a practice of your Christian life.

WHAT IS PRAYER?

It may help in learning how to pray to first become clear about what prayer is. Maybe it would help if we came to some definition about prayer. Too often the subject of prayer is clouded with misconceptions or no conceptions at all. So what is prayer? Let's consider several definitions that have served to be helpful. Prayer is "conversing with God as you would with anyone else." Prayer is "dialogue between two persons who love each other." Prayer is "communion between two kindred spirits." Prayer is "children talking to their Father." Prayer is the "finite communing with the Infinite: the creature communing with the Creator." Prayer is the "acknowledgment of our helplessness and the open expression of our need."

HOW CAN WE LEARN TO PRAY?

Now that we have some idea of what prayer is how can we go about learning to do it? The best way to learn how to pray is to start praying. No matter how awkward it may seem or how inadequate you may feel at first, start. Start sharing your life with God as you would with any concerned person. And as you do, be yourself – speak in your own words; don't be concerned about having some special prayer vocabulary. Be honest and open. Be frank and to the point. Don't be concerned about posture or the place or time when you pray. Simply start the practice of praying.

To teach us how to pray and what to pray for, a number of prayers by various individuals have been recorded in the Bible for our inspiration. David prayed an inspiring prayer in 1 Chronicles 29:10-14. Jesus gave us a model prayer in Matthew 6:9-13, and prayed what has been called his high-priestly prayer in John 17. The Apostle Paul offered prayer in five of his letters: Ephesians 1:15-23; 3:14-21; Philippians 1:9-11; Colossians 1:9-14; 1 Thessalonians 3:11-13; and 2 Thessalonians 1:11, 12. The letters of Hebrews and Jude close with prayers: Hebrews 13:20, 21; Jude 24, 25. A careful analysis of the content of these prayers could provide inspiration to enable anyone to start praying effectively.

We can further be helped in learning how to pray by listening to older, more mature Christians when they pray, provided we are cautious not to pick up their peculiar mannerisms and language styles.

ESSENTIALS TO PRAYER

In order for us to become effective in our praying there are several prerequisites that must be met. To begin with, we must approach God with *faith.* Hebrews 11:6 says it well: "Without faith it is impossible to please God, because anyone who comes to him must believe that he exists and that he rewards those who earnestly seek him." To receive anything from God we must believe in him and in his ability to grant our requests. This is fundamental to all praying.

A second prerequisite to effective praying is to pray all prayers *according to God's will.* Jesus teaches us to pray that way in the model he gave us when he taught us to pray, "Your kingdom come, your will be done." The Apostle John adds, "We have this assurance in approaching God, that if we ask anything according to his will, he hears us" (1 John 5:14). Many say the perfect prayer is the one Jesus prayed in the Garden of Gethsemane when he prayed, "not my will, but yours be done" (Luke 22:42).

To pray all our prayers according to God's will would obviously necessitate our knowing what his will is. So what is his will and how may we know it? God has revealed his will through his Word. So to pray according to his will we must know what he says in his Word.

A third prerequisite to effective praying is to pray with a *pure heart.* David says in Psalm 66:18: "If I had cherished sin in my heart, the Lord would not have listened." Solomon writes, "If anyone turns a deaf ear to the law, even his prayers are detestable" (Prov. 28:9). We cannot come to God with sin-stained hands or with ulterior or selfish motives and expect God to grant our requests. He will not be a party to our sin, selfishness, or self-seeking.

A fourth prerequisite to effective praying is to offer our prayers *in Jesus' name.* Jesus said, "You may ask me for anything in my name, and I will do it." And again, "the Father will give you whatever you ask in my name" (John 14:13; 15:16). What does it mean to offer our prayers "in Jesus name"? Is this some sure benediction that we can add at the end of our prayers that will guarantee our requests? No. References to someone's name in Scripture speaks of their nature or likeness. To pray in Jesus' name, therefore, is to pray consistently with all that we see in him. We could not, for example, pray for personal revenge, selfish ambition, for hurt or harm to come to another, or anything so unchristlike in "Jesus' name" because it would be inconsistent with who he is and what he stands for. So when we pray, we must always ask: "Can I honestly pray this in the name of Jesus?"

A final prerequisite to effective praying is to live a life of close intimate fellowship with Jesus continually, laying his word up in our hearts. He said, "If you remain (continue, abide) in me and my words remain in you, ask whatever you wish, and it will be given you" (John 15:7). Be assured of this: if we do as Jesus so directs, God will grant our prayer requests because we will not be asking for anything contrary to His will.

HINDRANCES TO PRAYER

Let's face it, establishing a daily routine of prayer is not something that comes easy. There are a number of things that work against it. For one thing it requires discipline and effort. It involves adding an extra block of time to what for many is an already crowded daily schedule. And since the time spent in prayer is in quiet physical inactivity, one can usually think of a dozen active things they could be doing to better use their time than to spend it in prayer. So to cease from all activity and spend time praying requires conviction, discipline, and effort.

Since in our pre-Christian lives we depended upon ourselves and our own effort to meet our needs, it may take some time before we come to the place where our helplessness and need drive us to pray for "our daily bread." And until we come to this place, our clinging in pride to our past sense of self-sufficiency will serve to hinder us from bringing our lives in daily prayer-dependency upon him who is indeed our all-sufficiency.

MOTIVATION FOR PRAYING

It is easy to see that for any of us to be motivated to carve a block of time out of our already crowded daily schedule and bow in quiet inactivity will require more than offering us a list of twelve reasons why we should pray daily. It would also take more than assuring us of blessings if we do. For us to establish a daily routine of prayer we are going to have to be highly motivated. And the motive is going to have to be more compelling than a list of reasons why we should pray, or a calculation of blessings that will be ours if we do, or a sense of duty, or blind obedience.

To be motivated to establish a disciplined life of prayer we must come to understand two basic things that are behind the whole idea of praying: what are we doing and what are we saying when we pause to pray?

For one thing, to pray is to acknowledge that God is God and we're not; and that we are entirely dependent upon him for everything temporal and eternal. Prayer is the denouncing of our own self-worship and the worshiping of God as the only true God. The root of all sin is the refusal to allow God to be God and create a god of our own making (Rom. 1:21). To worship God as God in prayer and acknowledge our absolute dependency upon him for everything and to seek to align our wills with his, is the essence of prayer and the prime motivation for engaging in it.

A second thing that is important to know about praying is that it is the means of expressing our thankfulness to God. The heathen world is characterized as being thankless. Paul the Apostle says that it neither glorifies God as God or gives "thanks to him" (Rom. 1:21). Most tribal people who have had no contact with the Biblical message of God do not even have a word for "thanks" in their vocabulary. Since becoming a Christian means to turn "to God from idols to serve the living and true God" (1 Thess. 1:9), this will mean forsaking the thankless life of our heathen past and spending the rest of life giving constant thanks to God for the continual flow of his love, grace, and goodness into our lives. Thankfulness must become a way of daily life. And the main way that thankfulness will be expressed will be in prayer.

The underlying motive for our spending time in prayer should be our love for God and our desire to tell him that we love him. When we come to see all that God has done for us in saving us and making every provision for both our temporal and spiritual lives, we will respond to his love by loving him. We will, as the Apostle John says, "love because he first loved us" (1 John 4:19). And our love will be verbally demonstrated in expressions of praise, adoration, and thanksgiving offered to him in prayer. If we genuinely love him, we cannot help but say so continually.

WHEN TO PRAY

The life of the believer should be lived in open conversation with God. It should be as in a telephone conversation where both receivers are off the hook and the line is open for continual conversation. Paul implied something like that when he wrote, "pray continually" (1 Thess. 5:17). Break into prayer at any time during the whole day. Pray at appointed times and as you are made aware of need. Paul wrote, "Pray in the Spirit on all occasions with all kinds of prayers and requests," and added, "be alert and always keep on praying . . ." (Eph. 6:18). Begin and end your day in prayer and pray all through the day. This is what Jesus did (cf. Mark 1:35; Luke 6:12; 5:16). Pray while you're exercising, bathing, and dressing in the morning. Pray while you're driving to and from work. Pray while you're cooking, doing dishes, ironing, and cleaning house. Pray while doing menial or routine tasks that require no thought. Pray during lunch or other work breaks. Pray as you are made aware of the needs of others throughout the day. Either pray with them or for them.

But lest your praying be determined by the people and events of the day, you need to have a fixed time and a place to meet with God to praise and thank him for his goodness and grace, seek his counsel and help for your life, and present the burden and concern you have for others. It is better to do this sometime at the beginning of the day and spend the day focused upon God, living in victorious dependency upon his grace and help than to go bungling through the day on your own and come to the end of the day seeking forgiveness for your failure.

May all of this serve in some way to aid you in developing a daily life of prayer that will enable you to experience intimate fellowship with God and become the recipient of the many blessings that come through a life of prayer.

4 Acquire a Christian Mentality

To live as a Christian necessitates a change in your mind and attitude from that of an unbeliever to that of a believer. Prior to becoming a Christian you acquired your value system and consequent lifestyle from the prevailing philosophies of the godless society you were brought up in and consequently you came to think as it thought and do as it did. And so far as God was concerned you were without knowledge and understanding, and your heart was hardened and insensitive (Cf. Rom. 1:21, 22; Eph. 4:17-19). But now that you have become a Christian all of that has changed. Your heart has become sensitive toward God and you have come to have a great desire to have his mind and do his will. So how can this desire be realized? By being reeducated in your mind with the truth of God. Or as the Apostle Paul puts it, "be made new in the attitude of our minds" (Eph. 4:23). He repeatedly calls upon the believer to acquire a Christian mentality as the means of being transformed into what God has called him to be in Christ (Cf. Rom. 12:2; Col. 3:10). In other words, if you're going to be a Christian and live like one, the first thing you're going to have to do is start thinking like one because we are all the product of our thinking. As Solomon says, "Above all that you guard, watch over your heart (Hebrew equivalent of mind), for out of it are the sources of life" (Prov. 4:23 Berkeley).

From day one we must determine to know all that we can about Jesus so that we can think as he does, see from his perspective, and therefore do as we saw him doing when he was in the flesh setting a pattern for us. He himself said, "learn from me," "do as I have done," follow my example (Matthew 11:29; John 13:15). And Paul wrote, "let this mind be in you, which was also in Christ Jesus" (Phil. 2:5 KJV).

ACQUIRING THE MIND OF CHRIST

How can we come to have the mind of Christ so that we think and act as he did? The mind of Christ is revealed in what he said and did. And the record of that is found in the four separate accounts of his life and ministry (Matthew, Mark, Luke, John) and what is said about him and his teachings in the letters of New Testament scripture. If his thoughts are going to be our thoughts and his life is going to be imitated by us, we are going to have to study those accounts until what they reveal to us becomes a permanent part of our thinking.

Knowledge of Christ and his way is something that each of us will have to acquire for ourselves. We will not inherit it from Christian family members. It does not come as a gift. No magical working of the Spirit will impart it to us. We will have to read and study to obtain it. And to be effective in our study we will need a few simple things.

YOU WILL NEED A GOOD BIBLE

The first thing we will need to help us acquire the mind of Christ will be a copy of the record that reveals it. Everyone will need a good, easy-to-read copy of the Bible. Secure a Bible in a language that you are used to reading daily. There are a number of them that could serve that purpose. There is the *New International Version*, *The New American Standard Bible*, *The New King James Version*, and the *New Revised Standard Version*, to list a few.

Choose a Bible with large bold print. Bibles with small, light print are a strain to read, fatiguing to the eyes, and do not make Bible study inviting. Get a Bible with wide margins on which you can make notes. Make sure it has good, solid backing on it because it's going to get a lot of use. And try to find one with heavy paper pages so that they can easily be turned and so that writing won't show through the pages.

YOU WILL NEED A BIBLE DICTIONARY

As you start studying your new Bible you will probably run across a lot of new terms referring to unfamiliar people, places, and things. To find their meanings you could go to a modern English dictionary, but you would find that many terms wouldn't be listed there. Even if they were the dictionary would give you the present-day meaning of the terms when you would want to know what they meant as used in Bible times. So what you will need is a Bible dictionary which will give you the meaning of terms as they were used in Bible times. Bible dictionaries come in one volume abridged editions as well as multiple volume exhaustive editions. Perhaps to start with you need a good one volume edition. There are a number of good ones on the market, for example, Unger's, Smith's, Davis's, and Revell. But if you would want an exhaustive set, the *Interpreter's Dictionary of the Bible* is a good five volume set.

A CONCORDANCE COULD BE HELPFUL

Another good help in reading and understanding the Bible is a Bible concordance. A Bible concordance is nothing more than a book that takes the words of the Bible, lists them alphabetically, and tells you all the places they appear in the Bible. A concordance can be very helpful in tracing down passages where you can only remember a phrase or a word. They can also be helpful in word studies because they will list for you all the passages where a particular word appears in the Bible. Like Bible dictionaries, concordances come in abridged as well as exhaustive editions and in either case they will be in one volume. Most study editions of the Bible come with an abridged concordance in the back. An exhaustive concordance would be the most useful and they are usually not much more expensive than an abridged edition. Most modern translations of the Bible have a companion exhaustive concordance. Two others are *Young's Analytical Concordance*, and *Strong's Exhaustive Concordance*, based on the King James Version.

A PLAN IS NECESSARY

Most people fail to establish a consistent pattern of Bible study because they are lacking in a plan. We humorously speak of those who let their Bible fall open, have their finger drop on a verse, and secure from it their counsel and direction for the day, or for their problem. But humor is often an exaggeration of real life. This would indicate that there are too many people who approach Bible study in that way. One of the main reasons people have not established a daily, disciplined, systematic study of God's Word is because they do not have a plan to discipline them to do so. A good plan for study can do as much as anything to help establish discipline. As long as you have a plan you are most likely to follow it.

There are many good plans that you can follow. A beginning plan for new Christians should be to read the New Testament through. To really get God's Word into your mind this could be followed by reading smaller books or sections of larger ones in their entirety every day for a month, changing translations each week. A good place to start this would be with Jesus' famous Sermon on the Mount (Matt. 5-7), which is a mandate for Christian living. This could be followed by the book of James which many have said is the easiest understood book in the New Testament and which is loaded with fundamental Christian truth. You could go on from James to Galatians to

Ephesians to Philippians and on, until you have gone through all the shorter books of the New Testament.

Other plans of study could include studying great Bible subjects such as faith, love, prayer, and fellowship. You could study the parables of Jesus which make up about one third of his teaching. You could have a study on his miracles, his personal conversations with people, his "I am" sayings – there's no end to what you could do to come up with a plan of study. But by all means establish a plan and then follow it.

YOU WILL NEED TIME

Because we live in such a busy age with its many duties and interests continually calling for our time, one of the problems most of us will face incorporating daily Bible study into our schedule is finding the time to do it. Since our days are already filled, the truth of the matter is that we will probably not find time – we'll have to make it. We will have to reshuffle our list of daily priorities so as to include it as one of the more important things to which we will give our daily time and attention.

We need to select a time when we will be most mentally alert, fix that as our time, and hold to it religiously. It will most likely be at the beginning of the day when we are fresh and alert rather than at day's end when we are worn out and our eyes have become heavy. Some have found first thing in the morning to be best. Others have incorporated it into breakfast time. Those who drive distances to work have utilized the time that takes to listen to cassette tapes of the Bible. Others have used their morning break or lunch period as a study time. Once we have seen the need and placed it high on our list of daily priorities, we will fix the time and place, and as we do, we will begin to acquire the mind of Christ.

5 You Cannot Be a Christian Without Belonging

The Bible makes it clear that Jesus must be loved, honored, served, and known in and through the members of his body, the church. For this reason it nowhere hints of anyone being a Christian apart from participation in the life of a caring, praying, sharing fellowship of believing men and women. It teaches that becoming a Christian means being gathered out of isolation into the corporate life of Christ's church.

The Bible knows nothing of a Christian being an island to himself. Its message of salvation is indissolubly bound up with its message of the church. Scripture never speaks of people being Christian apart from their being a part of the church.

> You cannot be a Christian without belonging. If you are in Christ, then you are joined to him and through him to all others who are joined to him. Salvation is not . . . being isolated in a hermetically sealed space capsule, but . . . being thrown together in community with a lot of other people chosen by God.[1]

The Christ who is presented as Savior is the Christ who is clothed with his body. There is no being reconciled to God without being reconciled to the people of God. One cannot be related to Christ without being at the same time related to the company of his disciples.

The biblical witness calling for believers to participate in the life of the church abounds in both the book of Acts and the epistles. Let the following twelve serve to illustrate:

---

[1]Michael Griffiths, *God's Forgetful Pilgrims*, p. 57.

TWELVE WITNESSES TO THE NECESSITY OF BELONGING

1. In 1 Corinthians 12:13 the apostle Paul writes, "We were all baptized by one Spirit into one body." About this George Ladd comments: "It is therefore impossible to be a believer and not to be baptized with all other believers into the body of Christ."[2]

2. From the beginning those who were won to Christ immediately became participants in the fellowship of believers and were added to their company. Luke describes the earliest converts to Christianity as those added to the number who had already become disciples. He writes in Acts 2:47, "And the Lord added to their number daily those who were being saved."

3. First-century believers are never pictured proclaiming the good news of Jesus to produce solitary faith and to scatter individual believers throughout the Mediterranean world. They went everywhere preaching the Word, making converts, and establishing churches. You need only to look at the ministry of Paul, the great missionary apostle, to see this clearly. Wherever he went, he left a trail of churches behind him. And in doing so he "showed that it was his conviction that from the very beginning Christianity must be lived in a fellowship. People were not left to be isolated individuals living alone."[3]

4. All the epistles of the New Testament are addressed to churches or groups of churches except four. And those four are written to give directions to three individuals regarding their ministries within the church and to the church. Even the book of Revelation is addressed to seven churches.

5. Nearly all instruction given to believers in the epistles is in the second person plural and should read "you all" for greater clarity. They speak of the Christian life only as it is lived in harmony with other believers. Indeed, there is no thought of anyone being able to live as a Christian apart from the fellowship and support of other believers. The epistles are, for the

---

[2]George E. Ladd, *The Theology of the New Testament*, p. 347.

[3]William Barclay, *The Acts of the Apostles*, p. 119.

most part, addressed to the "saints." P. S. Minear says, "Almost never is *hagios* (the Greek word for saint) used in the singular designating individual members of the church."[4] The epistles are not private letters to individuals to encourage them to live a solitary life. They are written to provide instruction for how to live in the community of believers. It is in the context of the fellowship of the church that God intends the Christian life to be lived.

6. God assigns spiritual gifts to individual believers to be utilized for the common good of all the members of His church, not for the personal gain of the individual. Spiritual gifts are meant to be used in harmony with, and complementary to, all other gifts. They do not work effectively, if at all, apart from their being orchestrated with other gifts. "The fact that the gifts of the Spirit are given to the people of God 'for the common good', i.e., for the contribution they make to the fellowship as a whole, means that an individualistic understanding of the gifts of the Spirit is ruled out."[5] The gifted men that Christ gave to His church after His ascension were "to prepare *God's people* for works of service, so that *the body* of Christ may be built up until *we all* reach unity in the faith" (Eph. 4:12, 13).

7. The most often used metaphor for the church appearing in the New Testament is "the body," with Christ as "the head." Not only does Paul say that "we were all baptized by one Spirit into one body," but he adds, "Now you (plural) are the body of Christ, and each one of you is a part of it" (1 Cor. 12:13, 27).

When Christ was on earth he had a human body through which he expressed the love of God. He was known as Jesus of Nazareth.Since his ascension, Jesus has manifested himself on earth through his human body, the church, made up of everyone who has united with his body. There is no separating the two and being joined to one while rejecting the other. Again George Ladd says, "In New Testament thought there can be no such thing as an isolated believer – a Christian who stands

---

[4]P. S. Minear, *Images Of The Church*, p. 136.

[5]Bruce Milne, *We Belong Together,* p. 58.

remote from other Christians. When he believes in Christ, he is made a member of Christ's body; he is joined to Christ himself and therefore to all others who in union with Christ constitute his body."[6]

8. Another metaphor which is used for the church in a way similar to "body" is "building." Paul says that believers were once "foreigners and aliens" to God but because of their faith in Christ they have become "fellow citizens with God's people and members of God's household, built on the foundation of the apostles and prophets, with Christ Jesus himself as the chief cornerstone. In him the whole building is joined together and rises to become a holy temple in the Lord. And in him you too are being built together to become a dwelling in which God lives by his Spirit" (Eph. 2:19-22). To become a Christian is to be joined to other Christians to form the temple of God. Christians are meant to be stones cemented together to form the walls of God's temple, not rocks lying about here and there.

9. The message of Ephesians, queen of the epistles, is that Christ "has destroyed the barrier, the dividing wall of hostility" that separates men one from another and has created a new humanity in which men are no longer alienated from one another due to hostility, but are bound together in love as "members of God's household," the church (Eph. 2:14-19).

10. In His high priestly prayer for His disciples (John 17), Jesus prayed that they might be bound together in a harmony and oneness comparable to the harmony and oneness of the Godhead. Unity and oneness were his final prayer concerns for the band of disciples and for all those who would believe in him "through their message."

11. Jesus said that the true badge of discipleship would be seen in his disciples' "love (for) one another." "One another" implies community. You can't express love to someone who isn't around. You will best express your discipleship by expressing your love toward those believers with whom you are living in fellowship.

---

[6]Ladd, *op. cit.*, pp. 542, 543.

12. Outside of the New Testament phrase, "in Christ," which is used more than sixty times by Paul alone, no other phrase is used more often than "one another." It appears fifty-six times in the Gospel of John, Acts, and the epistles. Its frequent use throughout all these writings serves to emphasize that most everything believers are called upon to do is to be done in relationship with "one another" – to and for and with "one another."

THE CHURCH, GOD'S INSTRUMENT

The purpose of the resurrection and ascension of Jesus and his sending the Spirit was to create a new people in history who would constitute His enlarged body, the church. This would enable him to reach out with God's love beyond the limits of a small group to the whole world. His three-and-one-half-year ministry in Galilee was only a beginning. It was only, as Luke puts it (Acts 1:1), what "Jesus *began* to do and to teach." The account in the book of Acts and all subsequent church history records what Jesus has continued to do and to teach by the Holy Spirit through his body, the church, "the fullness of him who fills everything in every way" (Eph. 1:23). To God "be glory in the church and in Christ Jesus throughout all generations, for ever and ever! Amen" (Eph. 3:21).

6 Why Christians Need to Meet Together Regularly

> Let us hold fast the confession of our hope without wavering, for he who promised is faithful; and let us consider how to stir up one another to love and good works, not neglecting to meet together, as is the habit of some, but encouraging one another, and all the more, as you see the Day drawing near (Heb. 10:23-25).

This admonition of Scripture was first given to a generation of Christians that was living during a time when severe persecution had begun to be directed toward the Church of Jesus Christ. Rome herself had declared war on Christianity and had designated Christians as enemies of the State. Their assemblies had been made a crime. Everywhere Christians were being sought out, brought before magistrates, and given the choice of recanting or dying. Yet in the face of all this, the Lord called upon Christians not to forsake the assembling of themselves together. Certainly in view of such circumstances this call to remain faithful in assembling must lend emphasis to the importance of Christians remaining faithful in every age. If ever there was a generation of Christians who had real reason for not assembling, it was the one which lived at the time of the writing of the letter to the Hebrews. If anyone would argue that Christian assembly is unnecessary or unimportant today, let him tell it to the martyrs of the first century who died in obedience to the Lord's admonition, "do not neglect to meet together."

From the day the church began through the period covered by Scripture we read that the first Christians regularly assembled together each week, and, in the beginning, every day. In Acts 2:42 we read that the first converts to Christianity "devoted themselves to the apostles' teaching and fellowship, to the breaking of bread and prayers" and that "*day by day*, attending the temple together" (2:46) they met for worship and study. We get a glimpse of the frequency of assembly of the Christians of Asia Minor when we read in Acts 20:7 that the Christians at Troas met "on the first day of the week." In 1 Corinthians 16:1, 2 we read of Paul giving direction concerning the Corinthian contribution for needy saints at Jerusalem. He directs them to put something aside and save "on the first day of every week," the obvious day of their regular assembly. In this we have both the admonition and example of Scripture calling Christians to regularly assemble on the first day of every week and on even more frequent occasions. Let us proceed to consider at least ten reasons why Christians should assemble each first day of the week and even more often.

TEN REASONS WHY CHRISTIANS ASSEMBLE

1. *Christians assemble each week to worship and praise the one, true, living God.* Since man is inherently a worshiping being, he is going to worship something. Either he is going to worship that which he has made with his own hands or that which is part of the creation of God. Whatever it may be he is going to worship something, and so long as it is anything other than the one, true, living God, it is idolatry. Our Christian faith is based upon our having "turned to God from idols, to serve a living and true God, and to wait for his Son from heaven, whom he raised from the dead, Jesus who delivers us from the wrath to come" (1 Thess. 1:9, 10). Christians assemble together to offer worship, praise, honor, and thanksgiving to the only true God who is the giver of "every good and perfect gift from above" (James 1:16).

2. *Christians regularly assemble together to show their love for Jesus Christ.* This indeed should probably be the first and prime reason why Christians assemble together. It isn't that they assemble under compulsion of some law or

regulation that forces them to do so, but rather out of simple love for their Savior who has done so much for them. They assemble together to prove their love for a Savior who "first loved them" (1 John 4:19). Each time a believer finds himself in the midst of a Christian assembly he should be able to say, "I'm here, blessed Lord Jesus, because I love you so much, and all the combined forces of hell could not keep me away."

3. *Closely akin to this, Christians assemble to remember Jesus Christ in a very special way in the Lord's Supper.* In an assembly with intimate disciples on his last night on earth, Jesus instituted the Lord's Supper as a means of remembering him in a very special way. He declared that as often as they partook of bread and the fruit of the vine that they would be remembering his suffering, death, and shame until he came again. He further said that this should be done "discerning the body" (1 Cor. 11:29), that is, perceiving that the body is assembled together and is doing this as a group. Seemingly the Lord's Supper was instituted as a special way for disciples to remember Jesus when assembled together as His Body, the Church.

4. *Christians regularly assemble together to show where their loyalty lies.* It is rather difficult to demonstrate your loyalty to Jesus Christ when you're in the same place doing the same things that non-Christians do when it is the appointed hour of Christian assembly. When Christians are assembled together on the Lord's day at the appointed hour of worship, they are letting their colors be unfurled and are demonstrating by their actions that they are on the side of the Lord Jesus Christ, standing for His program, His church and its ministry, and his Word and its proclamation. But when Christians are not to be found in the assembly on the Lord's day at the appointed time for any inexcusable reason, they are by their absence casting their vote to close the doors of the assembly hall, shut down all Christian education endeavors, and stop the proclamation of the gospel of Jesus Christ.

5. *Christians assemble together regularly as a token*

expression of their life's service. This means when a Christian gives two or three hours out of the 168 in a week to assemble for worship and study he is saying by giving that fraction, "Lord, I am offering to you my life, my devotion, my all in this hour of worship as an expression of the whole of my life which belongs to you every waking hour of my week." The term "services" as applied to the regular worship periods of the church is in reality a misnomer unless it refers to such worship as a token expression of the totality of life given to God in worship and service. For in reality, little, if any, actual service is offered to God by the assembly as a whole.

6. *Christians regularly assemble together for growth acceleration.* The repeated call of scripture is for Christians to "grow in the grace and knowledge of our Lord and Savior Jesus Christ" (2 Pet. 3:18). The Apostle Paul says, "Grow up in every way into him who is the head, into Christ," (Eph. 4:15) and again, "Him we proclaim, warning every man and teaching every man in all wisdom, that we may present every man mature in Christ" (Col. 1:28 RSV). The Hebrew writer issues the call, "go on to maturity" (Heb. 6:1). Now certainly the believer should be taking on some growth each day as in his personal devotion he searches the Scriptures and has fellowship with the Lord in prayer. But the Lord has made provision whereby he can take on accelerated growth in an additional way. Within the church the Lord has distributed various gifts of his grace among the various members. Some he has blessed with musical ability, some with ability to make money, others with the ability to serve well, and to some he has given the ability to teach and preach. To those whom he has given these abilities he has also given the ability to gain quick insight into his message so that they will have something to preach and teach. Therefore within the church there will also be teaching and preaching specialists able to gain quick insight into the meaning of the Word of God so that they can effectively communicate it to the church and bring each member to maturity much more quickly.

7. *Christians assemble together regularly to spur and incite one another to noble living.* In Hebrews 10:24 and 25 where the call is issued to Christians to regularly assemble themselves together, three reasons are cited for doing so. The first two reasons given are (1) "to stir up one another to love," and (2) "to stir up one another to good works." Did you ever stir up a red ant bed? If you ever have, you will know that ants begin moving about ten times faster than usual. The reason given for our assembling as Christians is to stir one another up in a similar manner so that we may be more active and productive in the two things that seem to epitomize our Christian faith, namely love and good works.

The third reason given for our assembling is to "encourage one another." Have you ever been down in the dumps as a Christian? If your answer is "no," you are certainly a rare specimen of a Christian, for most Christians do, at times, get down in the dumps. But the wonderful thing about it is that they don't all get that way at the same time. While one may be down in the dumps, another may be on the very top, able to lend a hand in lifting up the brother who is down. Now this is what happens when Christians get together in their assemblies. There may be some who may be very discouraged while at the same time there may be those who are at the height of exhilaration. The result is that those who are down are uplifted by those who are up. Have you ever gone to a worship service feeling blue, disappointed, and down in the dumps to find that the singing was edifying, the preaching was uplifting, and the fellowship was warm and encouraging? Before it was all over you felt lifted almost to the gates of heaven! That is being encouraged. As Christians, we don't live on the top all the time; we are not in the sunshine all the time. Sometimes there are dark clouds overhead. Sometimes we are at low ebb. The Christian life cannot be graphed as a straight upward rising line but must be graphed as an alternating up and down line with the mean reflecting a constant upward rise. There are times when we are up and there are times when we are down, and when we are down we need the encouragement of fellow Christians.

8. *We assemble together regularly as Christians because we are members of the body of Christ and our union with that body is vital to our spiritual life.* The Scriptures repeatedly contrast the church, the body of Christ, with the human body – a body composed of many members. With the parallel between the human body and the spiritual body of Christ being made so vividly in Scripture, and with spiritual conclusions being drawn on the basis of the similarity between the two, let us draw one. For example, let us take our right index finger. It is a member of our body in the same way that the believer is a member of Christ's spiritual body. Let us ask this question, "How long would our index finger live if it were severed from our body? "Only a few moments," you say, and you are right. Now if each believer is a member of the Body of Christ, how long do you think such a member could remain spiritually alive if he disassociated himself from the Body of Christ? "A relatively short time," you say, and again you are right.

9. *Christians gather together regularly for fellowship.* Since human beings are gregarious beings, they must have fellowship with their kind. Did you ever hear a child say, "I don't have anybody to play with!" And wonder why they said it? They say such things because they want fellowship. We all want it, we must have it; and we are going to get it somewhere with someone. Among the gregarious mammals we don't find apes fellowshipping with giraffes nor seals with polar bears. We find them all fellowshipping with their own kind. In the human family we don't expect Christians to be fellowshipping with members of the Hell's Angels but with other Christians. Christians get together to have fellowship with those of their own kind.

But fellowship involves more than just interaction between human beings – it is more than the sharing of personality with personality. Fellowship means to give or to share. Christians get together to give and to share not only of themselves but of their time, their money, their abilities, their all.

10. *Christians assemble together regularly for the employment of their gifts.* Christians do not assemble together merely to *get*, but also to *give*. They come together to mutually build one another up in the faith. And the most effective way this can be done is by every member employing the gift God has given them to minister. One comes to teach, another comes to help out financially, and yet another comes to serve and help out in whatever way he or she can. It is as all the members employ their gifts in service to one another that the whole church is kept healthy, strong, and active in the service of Christ.

WHAT HAPPENS IF WE NEGLECT THE ASSEMBLY?

Often someone will ask, "What would happen if I neglected to assemble regularly with fellow Christians?" Two Christians were sitting before the fireplace and the less mature had posed this same question to his more mature brother. Finding that words could not adequately supply the answer to the inquiry, the more mature brother picked up a poker and pulled one of the red hot coals out of the fire onto the hearth. In silence they sat watching it as it turned from red to pink to white to black and then died. In silence the question had been answered.

What would happen if you neglect to assemble regularly with the church? How long would your car be able to run on a battery that was not being regularly recharged? How long can a Christian hope to survive the drag of the world, the flesh, the devil, and the spirit of the times without being replenished by the edification received in the assembly of the church? It is utterly impossible to live the Christian life apart from the regular fellowship of the church. Those who live in neglect of the assembly and say, "Oh, we're still reading our Bible and praying. Our spiritual life is being maintained," are neither fooling themselves, God, nor anyone else. They are in the throes of spiritual death. If they are reading their Bibles at home as they say they are, what are they doing with Hebrews 10:24 and 25?

THE ASSEMBLY ORDAINED BY GOD

The church and its regular assembly has been ordained by God and God has nowhere ever instituted anything that was unessential or unnecessary for man's well-being. God designed the church assembly with its ministry because he knew it would be needed to sustain the spiritual life of his people. When someone says that the church and its assembly is unnecessary, they are saying that they know more about the needs of man than the God who made him.

HOW OFTEN SHOULD WE ASSEMBLE?

How often should we assemble? How often should we kiss our spouses in order to keep our love alive? How often should we take a bath to keep clean and remain inoffensive? The question, "How often should I meet with the church?" may be a question asked by one who is a babe in Christ seeking honest information. But more than likely it is the question of one who has grown cold toward the Lord and whose flesh is rebelling against what he considers to be an unnecessary ordeal.

Love does not concern itself with minimums, but with maximums. Love will not ask, "How often should I meet with the family I love?" Love will want to know, "How often am I going to be given the opportunity to gather together with my beloved brethren?"

How often should Christians assemble together? As often as they possibly can in large groups as well as small ones. The example of Scripture ranges from daily to every Lord's Day.

How often should Christians assemble together? How much growth does one need? How much strengthening does one's faith require? How much fellowship does life demand? How much love for Christ does one want to demonstrate? How often does one need to be spurred and incited to noble living? The honest answers to these questions will enable one to decide for himself how often he needs to assemble as a Christian.

7 Living Life in the Spirit

All of us start out in life as one-natured beings. We have a human nature which is bent upon doing what is human. The Apostle Paul says that our human nature is characterized by "gratifying the cravings of our sinful nature and following its desires and thoughts" (Eph. 2:3). In other words, the natural, normal human thing to do in life is to indulge your passions, desires, and your own thinking about things. To do such is not without serious consequence. And about that the Bible has much to say.

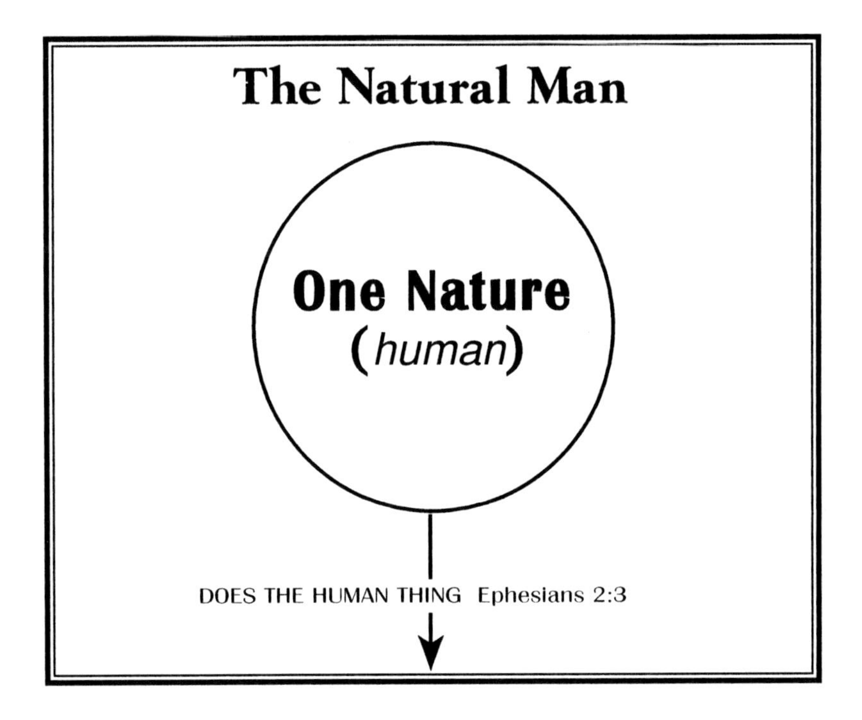

To become a Christian is to, as Peter puts it in 2 Peter 1:4, become a partaker "of the divine nature" and is to become a two-natured being. When one becomes a Christian, he retains his human nature but also receives a new nature from God. God "baptizes" or initiates him by putting his Spirit in his heart as a seal of his ownership of him (2 Cor. 1:22) and to provide him with the dynamic to enable him to become conformed to the image of Christ, his pattern Son.

THE INWARD TENSION OF THE CHRISTIAN

It is easy to see that when you have a nature bent on doing the human thing and another urging you to do the will of God you are going to experience inward tension because you're going to be pulled in opposite directions.

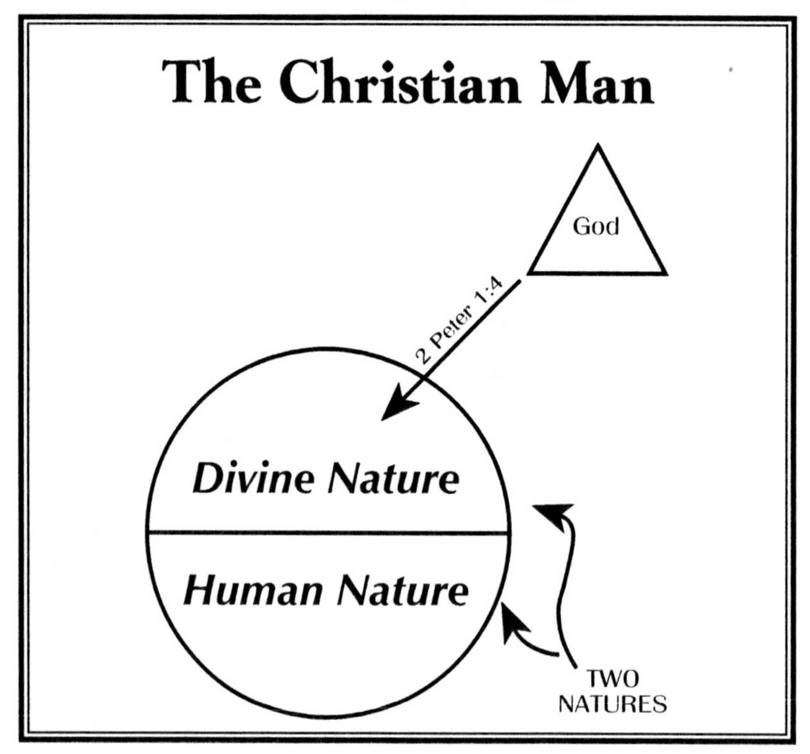

Paul puts it this way: "the sinful nature desires what is contrary to the Spirit, and the Spirit what is contrary to the sinful nature. They are in conflict with each other . . ." (Gal. 5:17). Ruth Paxson describes it as "war in your heart." New Christians experience this but seldom understand what's going on. They often think that becoming a Christian has introduced them into a strange world of inward turmoil. And in a sense it has. When they were unbelievers, their lives were only moving in one direction and there was no conflict. Now there is a pull in an opposite direction because God has begun to be at work within them. This creates inward tension. And this strange new tension is one of the surest signs that they have been born of God and are now spiritually alive.

As the Christian faces each life situation that calls for moral, ethical, or spiritual judgment and decision, he will experience an inner compulsion to do the natural, human thing which he has always done in the past. But at the same time there will be an inner coercion to do what Jesus did when he faced the same or similar situations.

Two strong influences will work upon the Christian encouraging him do the human thing. The human family, referred to in Scripture as the "world," will encourage, and sometimes pressure him, to conform to the human way of doing things. And the devil will lure and entice him to indulge himself – look out after his own best interests.

Two strong influences will be allied with his divine nature to aid him in doing the godly thing. The Word of God will provide him with the *counsel* of God. And the family of God, the church, will offer him *encouragement*. Whichever way he decides in each situation that he is faced with will determine which way his life will go at that instance.

Doing the human thing comes most naturally to us because we usually have been schooled in it the longest and, too, we are surrounded by those who are doing it constantly. Therefore to do the godly thing we must be continually "renewed in knowledge in the image of (our)

Creator" (Col. 3:10) or "be transformed by the renewing of (our) minds" (Rom. 12:2). In other words, we have to be schooled in God's way to learn what it is so that we can make godly decisions and walk in them.

But even when we learn what God would have us do, that does not necessarily insure that we will do it. Education alone is not enough. We will often find ourselves weak in desire and willpower to do what we know God would have us do. We need help in the desire and will departments to even begin to do God's will. Paul assures us that we have that help when he writes: "God is always at work in you to make you willing and able to obey his own purpose" (Phil. 2:13). About the only reason a believer can offer for not doing the known will of God in any instance is that he simply chooses to set God's will aside in favor of his own. He cannot plead weakness as he often does, because the full resource of God is available to enable him to execute on God's will if that is his choice. So if in any instance he chooses his own will over God's, his reason for doing so will have to be either rejection of it or, of course, ignorance of it in the first place.

Our own will is never overruled even though we are a partaker of the divine nature and have God at work in us to make us "willing and able to obey his own purpose." God is not at work in us to force or overrule our will but rather to undergird it. He is there to encourage and strengthen us to follow his counsel if that becomes our choice. But he does not override or take our will from us if we reject it. We must become convinced that what God has for us is the ultimate best, come to desire it in our hearts, "consider ourselves dead to sin and alive to God in Christ Jesus" (Rom. 6:11), and deliberately choose it for ourselves. When we do, he strengthens our faith and empowers us to then do what we want to do which will also be what he wants us to do.

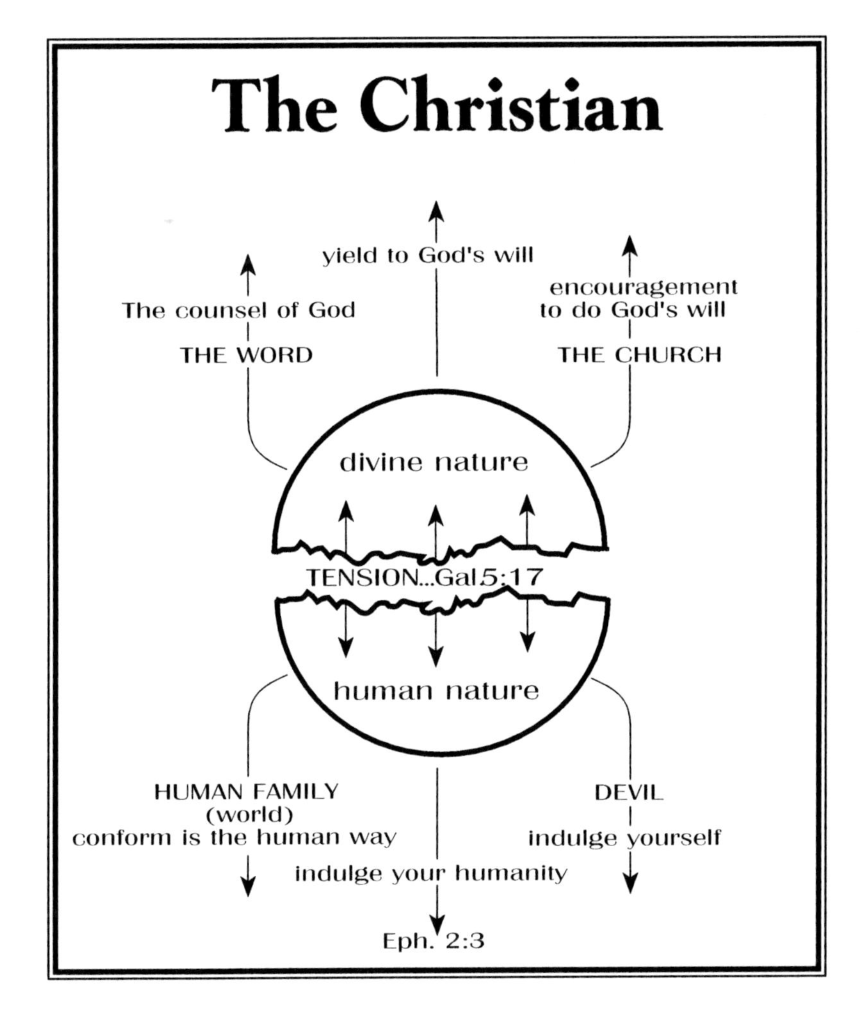

There are two ways we can go about rejecting God's will as it comes to us in each life situation. We can pour cold water on the counsel he would offer us and refuse to be led where he would take us, or we can out and out refuse his counsel in favor of indulging our humanity. The first of these the Bible calls "quenching the Spirit" (1 Thess. 5:19) and the second is referred to as "grieving the Spirit" (Eph. 4:30). Quenching the Spirit hinders forward progress in our spiritual walk because we reject the counsel that would move us forward. The Spirit is "grieved" when we reject the counsel of God and retreat to our pre-Christian way of living to indulge our passions and desires.

You can always tell when a believer has rejected the counsel of God and has temporarily returned to his former way of living. His sinful humanity will be evidenced in what the Bible calls "the works of the flesh" or "the acts of the sinful nature." Paul writes, "The acts of the sinful nature are obvious: sexual immorality, impurity and debauchery; idolatry and witchcraft; hatred, discord, jealousy, fits of rage, selfish ambition, dissensions, factions and envy; drunkeness, orgies, and the like" (Gal. 5:19-21).

ACCEPTING GOD'S WILL

When a life situation calls for an ethical, moral, or spiritual decision to be made and we accept God's counsel in the matter and proceed to do what he would have us to do, we will experience what the Bible calls "being filled with the Spirit" (Eph. 5:28) followed by "walking by the Spirit" (Gal. 5:16, 26).

To be filled with the Spirit means to come under the control of the Spirit or under the control of God. The context of Ephesians 5:18 makes this clear. It contrasts being filled with wine and being under its control with being filled with the Spirit and being under God's control. When in any life situation we yield to the counsel of God as it comes through his Word or is ministered through his people, we will in that instance be "filled with the Spirit" or will come under the Spirit's control. And because life is a series of situations coming one after another we are called upon to be "filled with the Spirit" repeatedly.

When we yield to the counsel of the Spirit and take a step in the direction that God would lead us, we are "walking by the Spirit." When we walk we take only one step at a time. When we walk with God we do so by making one decision at a time.

You can always tell when a believer has faced a situation

calling for a decision to "walk by the Spirit" or "gratify the desires of the flesh" (his human nature) and he has chosen to go with God. His decision to go with God will be evidenced in what the Bible calls "the fruit of the Spirit." Paul describes the "fruit of the Spirit" as being, "love, joy, peace, patience, kindness, goodness, faithfulness, gentleness, and self-control" (Gal. 5:22, 23).

In any given situation a believer can tell who is in control of his life – whether he's "walking in the flesh" or "walking by the Spirit" – by the kind of fruit that is being evidenced. And if it's not too clear to him, it certainly will be to others.

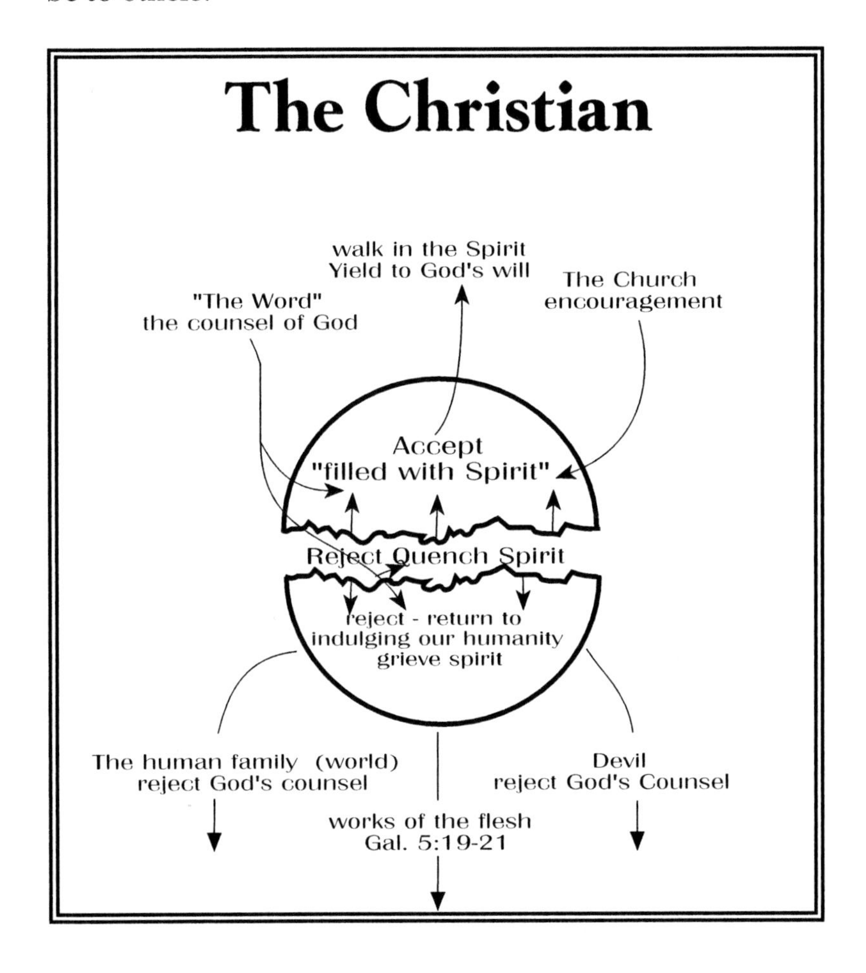

THE PLACE WHERE LIFE IS DETERMINED

The real issues of life are decided in the inner man where we make the decision either to be controlled by our human nature or by the divine nature; where we decide to "walk by the Spirit" or "gratify the desires of the flesh" (our human nature). There in the unseen quietness of our inner being our destiny is determined. Not in the "rah," "rah" hype of some big meeting or rally, but in the sanctuary of the soul. There the whisper of God comes in a still, quiet voice reiterating the wisdom and counsel of his Word that has been laid up in our hearts ready to be used for just such an occasion.

This is beautifully illustrated in Elijah's encounter with God at Mt. Horeb as it is related in 1 Kings 19. After having experienced a great spiritual victory at Mt. Carmel, out of fear from Jezebel's threat to kill him, Elijah fled over three hundred miles south to the refuge of a cave at Horeb. Believing that he was the only faithful believer left in Israel, he had come there to die. But God had something to say to him. He directed him to go out and stand on the mountain and there he would give him his word of counsel. A great and powerful wind arose with all of its power and fury and it shattered the rocks down the mountainside. But God "was not in the wind." Then came an earthquake with all its noise and power. "But the Lord was not in the earthquake." And after the earthquake came the fire of the Lord with all of its brilliance. "But the Lord was not in the fire." "And after the fire came a gentle whisper." God did not speak in all the fury and power and noise and brilliance of wind, earthquake, or fire. He spoke in a quiet, "gentle whisper." He whispered his counsel to Elijah: "Get up from here and go back home. I have some important work for you to do. And by the way, I have reserved seven thousand men in Israel who have not bowed the knee to Baal or kissed him."

That's how God still counsels us as His people and directs our lives. In the unseen quietness of the inner man he brings his written word, which has been laid up in our hearts, to our conscious attention and urges us to do what it says.

Let me illustrate this in an experience that would picture the inner conflict between our two natures.

One morning as I came to work I parked my car and walked along the side yard of one of my fellow workers. His wife and two children were outside in the yard and I could see that they were just beginning to paint a number of very large boxes. She had a brush in her hand that looked to be about two inches wide. Not knowing that she was only showing one of the children how to paint so that they could participate, and thinking that it was going to take her all day to paint the boxes with such a small brush, I inquired, "You're not going to paint all those boxes with that small brush, are you?" (I had planned to go home and get her a bigger one if she was.) But she replied, "Don't get on my case this morning! I had a rough night and I'm not up to it!" Well, like a dog that had been kicked, I put my tail between my legs and went into my office. Being a significant other in my life, her reply had so wounded me that I couldn't sit down and go to work. I just stood there dazed, looking out the window thinking about what had just transpired. I thought to myself, "I've got to do something. I can't stand here all day. What shall I do? How shall I respond to this injury?" The first thought that came to my mind was, "From now on I'll avoid walking by her yard so that I won't suffer any more injuries like this." Then a second thought came: "And I'll never ever again consider doing anything for her unless she begs me." Then it struck me, "This is a typical human response. This is my human nature exerting itself. And I'm not going to do the human thing in this situation. I'm going to consider myself dead to the old human way and execute on my Christian conviction." Then I asked, "What should my Christian conviction be in a situation like this?" Immediately, 1 Peter 4:8 came to mind, and it was as if God whispered his counsel to me: "Above all, hold unfailing your love for one another, for love covers a multitude of sins." I considered that for a moment and then concluded: "She's never been like that before. She's always been a close, loving friend. This is an exception, not the rule. I'm going to continue to walk by her yard. And whenever I see her needing help and I can assist, I'm going to offer to help." Peace came to my heart immediately and I sat down and went to work. As I did I had an inkling that God was stirring in her life at the same time.

About thirty minutes later there was a soft knock on my office door. I said "Come in." A hand reached through the partially opened door with a delicious looking pastry in it. A voice coming from one still outside said, "I've brought a peace offering." I said, "Come on in." My friend's wife entered and I asked her to be seated. She began to relate the inward turmoil she had experienced after abruptly replying to me and how God had compelled her to repent and come make an apology to me. I shared what I had just gone through and we both praised the Lord that we had been led to yield to His counsel and "walk by the Spirit." That, I am convinced, is how God would have us meet each life situation and respond to it whether we always do or not.

8 What It Means to Be Filled With the Holy Spirit

To everyone who receives Jesus as Savior, God grants the potential for a completely new and different life. In biblical terms, he gives them a gift, the gift of his Holy Spirit. In the previous chapter we noted that one of three things can be done with this great potential for new life. You can ignore it and life can go on the same old way as though nothing had happened. You can refuse to let it be realized in your life. Or, you can open up your life to the full realization of the new potential and enter into a new sphere of living. The Bible puts it this way: you can "grieve the Holy Spirit" "quench the Holy Spirit," or "be filled with the Holy Spirit." The believer responds to the Holy Spirit in one of these three ways every waking moment of his life. Let's elaborate on each one of them to make sure that our understanding is clear.

DO NOT GRIEVE THE HOLY SPIRIT

In Ephesians 4:30 the apostle Paul writes, "do not grieve the Holy Spirit of God." To grieve means to cause sorrow or remorse. How? The context of this passage shows us. God is grieved when the believer surrenders to sin instead of to him. In Ephesians 4:24-32, the context surrounding the directive "do not grieve the Holy Spirit," we have Paul saying, "eliminate from your life lying, anger, stealing, evil talk, bitterness, wrath, clamor, slander, and malice." These are a sampling of the types of things that cause grief to the Holy Spirit. When Paul says "do not grieve the Holy Spirit of God" he is saying, "do not surrender to and follow after sin because to do so is not only injurious to you but it causes God grief."

DO NOT QUENCH THE HOLY SPIRIT

In 1 Thessalonians 5:19 Paul directs, "do not quench the Spirit." Whereas to *grieve* the Holy Spirit is to ignore Him and actively participate in sin, to *quench* the Holy Spirit is to refuse to listen to His positive direction for life. It is to throw water on and dampen the fires that he would build in our lives for truth and righteousness and service. It is to respond to the suggestions of the Holy Spirit with such rebuff as "I don't feel like doing that," "I don't want to do that," "I would rather do something more exciting or more important," "I don't think I'm the right one for the task." So long as you take this attitude toward the urging and directing of the Holy Spirit you will not be led to be or to do what the Spirit wants you to.

BUT BE FILLED WITH THE HOLY SPIRIT

It is not God's will that the believer live a life of either grieving or quenching the Holy Spirit. He would rather have him "be filled with the Holy Spirit" (Eph. 5:18). What does it mean to be filled with the Holy Spirit? The context in which this passage is found will help us to understand. Being filled with the Spirit is contrasted with being filled with an intoxicant. Paul writes "Do not get drunk with wine . . . ; but be filled with the Spirit." In a sense he is saying that life in the Spirit is something like being under the influence of alcohol. As in drunkenness where one is filled with alcohol and therefore comes under its influence and control, so it is with the Spirit. One who is filled with the Spirit comes under his influence and control. In other words, as you can turn your life over to liquor and become liquor controlled, so you can turn your life over to God and become God controlled. The godly life results from being God controlled.

To be filled with the Spirit is not the same as being filled with emotion. To be filled with the Spirit calls for an exercising of the will, because "being filled with the Spirit" is a command. The command is literally "be being filled with the Holy Spirit," involving one in continued, sustained action. God is not seeking an emotional response from man but a volitional one. If at the beginning of football season the football coach, seeking to get all his players in shape, says at the beginning of each day's practice, "Okay fellas, let's get out and run around the track three times to warm up," the players are not going to stand there with tears running down their cheeks responding emotionally. Their response will be to obey. They will exercise their will by getting on the track and running around three times as the coach has directed. The "Spirit filled" or "God controlled" life will result when one exercises his will in obedience to what God directs for his life. To have this understanding of what it means to be filled with the Holy Spirit is to remove the air of mystery and mysticism that has sometimes surrounded it. There is nothing mysterious about the fact that God wants to have control of your life. Letting God control your life is not going to lead you into any kind of mysticism.

THE SPIRIT FILLED LIFE

What will result in your life if you are filled with the Holy Spirit? Will you immediately be thrust into spectacular projects or ministries for God? Will you be rushed off to evangelize Borneo? Will you start holding city-wide gospel crusades? Will your life become surrounded with the miraculous? Not very likely. Not according to the context in which the command for being filled with the Spirit is found.

God is extremely practical and we can love him all the

more for it. When God calls upon us to be filled with his Spirit or come under his control, he immediately starts dealing with life where we are living it. He starts picturing life for us as he would have it lived in its most common ventures. To see this just keep on reading what follows Ephesians 5:18.

WE WILL BURST FORTH IN SINGING

First of all, in verse 19 Paul says that if you are filled with God's Spirit you will have a new song in your heart. The new freedom and release that you experience as a result of turning your life over to God's direction will cause you to break forth in singing.

EVERY DAY WILL BECOME THANKSGIVING

Secondly, Paul says that when God takes over the control of your life it will become a life of thanksgiving. The old life of negativism, grumbling, complaining, and fault-finding will be replaced with a new life of thanksgiving and praise. Instead of complaining about everything, you'll start giving thanks to God for what you already have and for what you know He is going to continue to give. As the old hymn says, you'll start counting your blessings and naming them one by one: "Thank you, Father, for life; thank you, Father, for health; thank you for food in abundance and for family and loved ones in Christ and for the great salvation which you have given to me and for the tasks that you have given me to perform, etc." To have a new song in the heart and to enter into a life of thankfulness could in itself revolutionize the lives of most modern saints. But Paul goes on.

WE WILL BECOME SUBJECT TO ONE ANOTHER

In the third place, Paul says in verse 21 that those who are filled with the Holy Spirit will be subject to one another. You will begin to become concerned about meeting needs in the various relationships of life. Husbands will become concerned about meeting the needs of their wives. Wives will become concerned about meeting the needs of their husbands. Parents will become concerned about meeting the needs of their children. Children will begin honoring their parents. "Dad, I just mowed and edged the lawn. What else do you have for me to do?" "Mom, I know you're tired from ironing all afternoon and from cooking dinner. Just sit down in the den and relax, I'll clean up the table and do the dishes." Wow! Is that what it means to be filled with the Holy Spirit? Yes!

WIVES WILL BECOME SUBJECT TO HUSBANDS

In the fourth place, Paul says in verses 22-24 that when wives are filled with the Holy Spirit they will become subject to their husbands in everything. There isn't any reason to believe that it is natural for women to be subject to their husbands in everything. They have an ego just like everyone else. It is natural for them to have their own way and be subject to no one. And after all, "haven't they come a long way?" Now, of course, it is easier for some women to be subject to their husbands than others, because some women have a "neat hubby." But ultimately it is only when a women is under the influence of the Holy Spirit that she can be truly subject to her husband in everything. This subjection is something between her and God. She becomes subject to her husband because she has committed herself to do what God directs for her life. Men cannot use this passage to attempt to force their wives into subjection to themselves. It just won't work. It wasn't meant to work that way. This is a directive from God to wives who are submitting themselves to his control.

HUSBANDS WILL CARE FOR THEIR WIVES

In the fifth place, Paul says in verse 25 that when husbands are filled with the Holy Spirit they will love their wives enough to be willing to die for them. It is interesting to note that the word for love in this passage is *agape* and not *eros*. God is not saying that if a man comes under his control he will speed up the tempo on his erotic love for his wife, but that he will start giving himself to her to meeting her needs and building her up. It is easy to see that when a woman knows that her husband loves her enough to be willing to give his life for her that there will be little difficulty in her surrendering herself to his leadership.

CHILDREN WILL HONOR AND OBEY PARENTS

In the sixth place, Paul says in Ephesians 6:1-3 that when children, or youth in the household, are filled with the Holy Spirit, it will result in their obeying their parents and honoring them as the leaders of the family. This doesn't mean that children must acknowledge that their parents are always right in everything, but that they are God's appointed authority over the home in the power structure that He has set up. When parents know that their children are living in obedience to their authority a beautiful relationship will result between them. Let's see how it might work. "Dad, can I borrow the car tonight to take Mary to the football game? And afterwards, we'd like to go to the drive-in for a hamburger and a hot fudge sundae and then I'll take her home." "What time will you be coming home?" Dad asks. "Well, Dad, we won't get away from the game till about 10:30 and there will be a crowd at the drive-in, oh – I guess I'd be home about midnight." The father replies, "I want *my* car in *my* garage at 11:30 and that is final." Now right here is where a young person can blow it if he is not under the control of the Holy Spirit. He could say, "Dad, keep your stinking car, I'll never ask you for it again as long as I live." But if he is under the control of the Holy Spirit he might reply something like this, "Dad, I know it's your car and that it is a privilege for me to get to use it and don't think I don't appreciate it. And if you want the car home at 11:30, well, it'll be home at 11:30, because you're the dad." What happens to a father after an experience like that? He probably goes through an agonizing day thinking over this transaction so that night the scene might go like this: "Son, here's the keys to the car. You and Mary go to the football game and have a good time and come home at a reasonable hour." The father knows that the son is subject to him and that he can trust him to do what is right, so there is no conflict, no problem.

FATHERS WILL LEAD THEIR CHILDREN

In the seventh place, Paul says in Ephesians 6:4 that fathers who are filled with the Holy Spirit will not provoke their children to wrath, but bring them up in the discipline and instruction of the Lord. Why fathers? Because they're the God-appointed responsible leaders of the family. They're the C. E. O. of the corporation. The mother is the chairman of the board.

Holy-Spirit-filled fathers do not pick at, bug, or provoke their children, keeping them angered all the time. But they will do the things that will serve to bring their children up in the discipline and instruction of the Lord. "Discipline" refers to personal example. Its root is the word "disciple." The inference is that parents filled with the Holy Spirit will live such exemplary Christian lives before their children that they will turn them on for Christ. Here is where so many church members' kids are turned off. They look at their parents who profess to be Christian and they see no Bible study, no prayer, no witness, no anything in their lives that witnesses of Christ. And it turns them off. They see their parents as phonies. That's why we have a lot of confused spiritual kids around the church. But when parents are really living the life and have the respect of their children, they are able to give them verbal instruction about the Lord. You will listen to someone if you have respect for him.

ALL WORK WILL BE DONE FOR CHRIST

In the eighth place, God says that if a worker is filled with the Holy Spirit he will work on his job at whatever he does as though his boss was Jesus Christ himself (Eph. 6:5-8). He won't work just when the boss is around, he won't work for ulterior motives or reasons; he'll work faithfully and honestly at all times as though rendering all to Christ. When Christian workers become responsible workers like that, they should inevitably advance to positions of leadership and high pay. God doesn't expect His people to stay at the bottom of the totem pole in their work. He teaches them that they should prosper. In 3 John 2, John writes "Beloved, I pray that in all respects you may prosper and be in good health, just as your soul prospers"(NASB). Of course, this is premised on the Kingdom being first (Matt. 6:33).

This applies just as well to students in school as it does to workers on the job. Students who are filled with the Holy Spirit will be doing their very best in their studies. They will make the best grade that their ability will permit. They will be laboring in their studies as though Christ was the school principal or superintendent.

EMPLOYERS WILL BECOME THE EMPLOYED

In the ninth place, Paul says that employers who are filled with the Holy Spirit will run their businesses always bearing in mind that they too are in the employment of another (Eph. 6:9)

OUR STRENGTH WILL BE FOUND IN GOD'S PROVISION

And finally, Paul says that when one is filled with the Holy Spirit he will find his strength in the Lord utilizing everything that he has made available to him to resist all attacks from the devil and stand firmly in his faith in Christ.

These are the common ventures of life and it is here that the filling of the Holy Spirit will have primary application. It will be from a solid base developed in these areas that God will direct us into greater ventures. But until he has had his way here we are not prepared to attempt greater things. You cannot go on to greater things in Christ when your personal life, your family life, and your work life has no real witness of Holy Spirit control.

9 The Blessing of Trials

Becoming a Christian doesn't mean that all our troubles will cease. God doesn't put us in a hothouse to shelter us from the adversities of life; neither does he change the world we live in so that it starts accommodating us. No, the change that God effects takes place within us. The new life that he generates within us gives us a potential to meet the difficulties and trials of life head-on, work through them, and emerge the better for the experience. We will be pruned of destructive life patterns of the past, purified in faith, strengthened in character, and made more mature and complete in Christ.

TRIALS ARE SURE TO COME

The Bible repeatedly warns us that we are sure to face trials as long as we live in this world. In Job 2:10 Job asked, "Shall we accept good from God, and not trouble?" Later on, Jeremiah asked a similar question, "Is it not from the mouth of the Most High that both calamities and good things come?" (Lam. 3:38). In Job 5:7, Eliphaz said, "Man is born to trouble as surely as sparks fly upward." And in Job 14:1, Job said much the same thing: "Man born of women is of few days and full of trouble." Early in his ministry Jesus exhorted his disciples not toworry about the future saying, "Each day has enough trouble of its own" (Matt. 6:34). Some of the parting words he spoke to his disciples the night before the cross were, "In this world you will have trouble" (John 16:33). The writer of Hebrews asks, "What son is not disciplined by his father? If you are not disciplined (and everyone undergoes discipline), then you are illegitimate children and not true sons" (Heb. 12:7, 8). He goes on to add, "Our fathers disciplined us for a little while as they thought best; but God disciplines us for our good, that we may share in his holiness" (Heb. 12:10). James begins his letter by saying, "Consider it pure joy, my brothers, whenever [not "if"] you face trials of many kinds" (James 1:2).

Actually, to become a Christian will probably mean that you will experience more adversity than usual because becoming a Christian will result in your beginning to experience the trial of persecution. This may start coming upon you, as Peter warns in 1 Peter 4:12, "as though something strange were happening to you." But Jesus forewarned about this in John 15:20, 21 as he sought to prepare his disciples for life without him: "No servant is greater than his master. If they persecuted me, they will persecute you also . . . They will treat you this way because of my name, for they do not know the one who sent me." He offered further explanation in a prayer he prayed for them in John 17:14, "I have given them your word and the world has hated them, for they are not of the world any more than I am of the world."

Upon becoming a Christian you may experience something similar to what Nadine did. Nadine was a waitress in a large restaurant. She was the most popular person that worked there. For several months she had been studying the Bible considering the claims of Christ. This resulted in her receiving him as her Lord and Savior and making her acceptance public before the world in baptism one Sunday morning in the assembly of her local church. The following morning she unhesitatingly shared what she had done with all her fellow workers and told them of the new joy and peace that had come into her life. She was unprepared for the response this brought. She couldn't understand it. One day she had been the most popular person in the restaurant whose company people constantly sought, and the next day she became an enemy whom everyone began to shun.

What had happened to create such a turnabout? She had brought Christ into their midst and they were reacting to him in their enmity. They were treating her the way they did because she now represented him and was no longer a part of their world.

If you take your stand for Christ in this world you will repeatedly experience what Nadine did. In fact, you need to know that "everyone who wants to live a godly life in Christ Jesus will be persecuted" (2 Tim. 3:12). But don't become discouraged when it happens to you. It will serve to verify the reality of your Christianity, put you in company with the greatest saints of all time – including Jesus, and bring the promise of a great reward in heaven (Cf. Matthew 5:12).

OUR NORMAL, HUMAN REACTION TO TRIALS

How I wish some mature believer had taken me aside when I was a new Christian and helped me to see the important part difficulties and trials play in the development and maturing of a believer. I don't think I would have resisted and fought against them so, and I am sure I would have grown much more rapidly.

But not knowing their purpose in God's plan for maturing the believer, I looked upon trials as any ordinary man of the world would have. I saw no purpose in them, no good coming from them, and that they were something to be avoided at all cost. I saw them serving only to cause me inconvenience, extra work, trouble, hurt, and pain. And I didn't want any of that. So when adversity came I typically responded by asking, "Who needs this! Why is this happening to me, especially at this time? What did I do to deserve this? Haven't I gone through enough already?" And I did everything I knew to get out of the trouble or mess I was in. And because I did, I found myself going through the same thing over and over. Later, I came to see that I was bound to do that because God couldn't take me to the next level of maturity until I had learned the lesson at hand. God doesn't operate like so many of our public school systems do. He doesn't push us along to a higher level whether or not we have learned anything. No, good Parent that he is, he will not take us to a higher level until we have learned what we need to know where we are presently.

When our children were young my wife and I didn't let them go outside and play in the busy city we lived in until we felt sure they would stay within the bounds and limits we set for them. So how did we come to such an assurance that convinced us that we could give them this new experience of freedom? We tested their obedience in the house prior to their going out. When we felt they had passed the tests there, then we let them go out. But not until then.

God wants to lead us to ever higher levels of maturity and greater experiences of freedom. And one of the main ways he does this is through the discipline of trials and adversity. If we learn what he thinks we need to know from one experience he will move us on to the next. If for whatever reason we don't learn what he has designed for us to learn, we will be bound to repeat the course until we do.

At the time it may seem painful and repetitious to do this but it is a necessary procedure we must go through in order to come to maturity. It is somewhat like scaling a steep mountain. You get to the top by going through much painful, repetitious difficulty.

The lessons that I have learned best since becoming a Christian are those that I have learned through the painful experiences brought on by trials and adversity. Disneyland experiences have taught me little or nothing.

THE PURPOSE OF TRIALS

Though difficulties and trials may result in painful experiences to go through, if at their onset we can accept them as opportunities to have our faith developed and can see them as a means for taking us to a higher level of maturity and completeness in Christ, we will not fight against them or try to avoid them but we will rejoice in them because they will be providing us opportunities to grow.

Trials are meant to be our servants, not our enemies. God seeks to use them in our lives to work for our ultimate good (Rom. 8:28). He wills that they serve to bless us and not curse us. He permits them for our benefit; not to make us weaker but stronger, not to defeat us but for us to defeat them; not to make us fall, but to make us soar. But unless we can see their purpose as he does, we will continue to seek to avoid them at all cost, chafe under them if they come upon us, and gain nothing from them after we have experienced them. So it would seem important to have some idea of how they can serve to bless us. Let's consider several ways in which God intends for them to do that.

THE BLESSING OF TRIALS

For one thing, trials serve to prove the genuineness of our faith. Peter wrote in 1 Peter 1:6, 7, "In this you greatly rejoice, though now for a little while you may have suffered grief in all kinds of trials. These have come so that your faith – of greater worth than gold, which perishes even though refined by fire – may be proved genuine . . . ." Peter is saying that as firing removes impurities from gold, so trials purify faith. How? By removing everything unessential to it. Trials compel us to forsake all that we have embraced that is superfluous to our faith, and contend only for that which is vital – that which we would consider worth suffering or dying for. When this happens to us we will arrive at a more genuine faith.

James says when we know the ultimate outcome of trials, we can actually face them with rejoicing (James 1:2, 3). He pictures the ultimate as being maturity and completeness in Christ. He goes on to say that "trials" are the "testing" that develops the conquering, enduring spirit (literal meaning of "perseverance") that leads us to it. He concludes (1:12) that "the man who perseveres under trial" is "blessed," "because when he has stood the test, he will receive the victor's crown, the life God has promised to those who love him." William Barclay comments "that if the Christian meets the trials and the testings and the temptations of life in the steadfast and unswerving constancy which Christ can give, then life becomes an infinitely more splendid thing than ever it was before."[1]

The Apostle Paul joins James in saying that "we can be full of joy here and now even in our trials and troubles" (Rom. 5:3, Phillips) when we know what their end result will be. Like James he says that they produce "perseverance," but adds that perseverance produces "character; and character hope." The term he uses for "character" is taken from a word that describes metal which has been purified by passing through a purging fire. He is saying that the trials and pressures of want and need, of difficult circumstances, sorrow, persecution, rejection, and loneliness must not be looked upon as meaningless hardships set to discourage and destroy us, but as opportunities provided by God to make us a better, stronger, purer person better able to draw nearer to him.

The author of the book of Hebrews writes to inform us that believers will most assuredly experience difficulties in their lives which will be used by God as a discipline to produce holiness, righteousness, and peace within (Heb.12:5-11). Their coming will be a sure witness that He loves us and that we are his true children "because the Lord disciplines those whom he loves," and in his so doing He is treating us as "true sons." Of course the discipline will be a "painful" thing to experience while we are going through it, as is all discipline, but it is needful that we "endure" it, the writer exhorts, because "it produces a harvest of righteousness and peace for those who have been trained by it."

---

[1] Barclay, *The Letters of James and Peter*, in *The Daily Study Bible*, p. 58.

A FINAL WORD OF ENCOURAGEMENT

Even though we may know that trials are permitted by God for a beneficial purpose and that without them we could never reach the degree of maturity that He is calling us to in Christ, they may at times become so intense and painful and so seemingly unending that we will conclude that we can no longer endure them. God anticipated that this might happen to us and therefore has given us his word of assurance (1 Cor. 10:13) that we will never be tried beyond our ability to survive. He promised in his faithfulness that he would not let us "be tempted[2] beyond what we can bear." He further promised that when the trial becomes too intense, "he will also provide a way out so that (we) can stand up under it." And he assures us that whatever our trial may be, it will never be ours alone but the sharing of the common experience of other believers. To know this can, in itself, comfort and encourage us, and to then share our experience with other believers will serve to encourage us even more.

So do not fight against trials as though they were enemies come upon you to harm or destroy you, but receive them as friends sent by God to discipline and bless you. And do so with the confidence that no matter how intense they may become, they are being regulated by Him and He will not let them exceed your ability to endure.

---

[2]The word translated "temptation" and "tempted" in 1 Corinthians 10:13 is the very same Greek word translated "trials" in James 1:2, 12.

10 "Say Goodbye to the Feelings"

Before we became Christians we pretty much did what we felt like doing. What we did was determined more by our feelings than by any sense of a compelling conviction. Most of life was lived for the moment as we sought after what seemed to offer the most pleasure and satisfaction and what appeared to be wisest and most expedient for us. We only did what we chose to do unless, of course, there was some constraint upon us to do otherwise. So if we felt like being helpful to others we were, but if we didn't feel like it, we weren't. In reality, we lived under the control of our feelings. We followed their every whim.

THE PROBLEM WITH FEELINGS

But now that we have become Christians we can no longer live under the control of our feelings. If we continue to do what pleases us we will not do what pleases Jesus. Everything he leads us to do will have to first satisfy our feelings or we won't do it. If he calls upon us to get up on Sunday morning and join other believers in worship and we don't feel like doing it, we'll stay in bed. If he calls upon us to a time of daily, disciplined prayer and we don't feel like praying some days, we won't. If he urges us to share our faith with others and we feel like it might get us into an embarrassing situation, we won't do it. So in reality, instead of Christ ruling over our lives, our feelings will still be in control.

If we continue to live by our feelings as Christians we can expect to get into some serious difficulties. For one thing, we can become an easy prey of the devil. Following our feelings can give him an opportunity to manipulate us. When he knows that our sense of well-being is dependent upon our feeling good, he can bring about situations and circumstances that can make us feel so bad that we will even doubt our salvation.

And another thing, living by our feelings can at times lead to insecurity, and at other times lead to a false security in our position in Christ. When we base our security in Christ on our feelings we are in for a roller coaster experience. One day we may believe that we are secure in Christ because we feel so good. And the next day we may even doubt that we are a Christian because we feel so low and miserable.

To live by feelings can lead to an irrational, illogical, unreasonable faith and can even make God out to be inconsistent, ignorant, and immoral.

I have a Christian friend who at times is given to following his feelings instead of the wisdom of God's word. On one occasion he got emotionally stirred to go to one of the French South Sea islands to be a missionary. He was sure it was the call of God. He quit his good job, liquidated his assets and flew to Hawaii with his family where he planned to get the necessary visas to immigrate and gather together what would be necessary to equip himself and his family to be effective missionaries. But when he went to the French Consulate to get the visas, the French wouldn't issue them. So he ended up returning home again where he had to get a new job and start all over again.

This is the kind of situation you can get into if you follow your feelings and mistakenly equate their promptings as the leading of God. It can make God appear to be ignorant, not knowing what he's doing from one day to the next. And it can make him out to be immoral for putting his people through such unnecessary ordeals.

We need to be aware that our feelings can be affected by many variables: the state of our mental and physical health, how others greet us and what they say to us, the weather, conditions at work or at home, good or bad news. If we allow our feelings to be our guide, what we do with our lives will be determined by every situation or person that comes along.

There is one more problem you may face if you live by your feelings. You may not always have any to keep you going. There will come times when it will seem as though they've gone away. And if you've been living in dependency upon them, you may easily conclude that you've lost your Christianity. Twila Paris anticipates times like these in her song "If The Feelings Ever Go Away" when she sings: "If the feelings ever go away I will keep on choosing to obey you."

You will probably have few problems in following the Lord when the sun is up and all is going well. But what about when the sun doesn't shine? What about times when you're emotionally down? And we all have those times. We all experience spiritually dry times. Times when it seems like what began with such excitement and enthusiasm at conversion has run its course, faded away, and left us. We can become so emotionally drained and empty that we may even feel like throwing in the towel. Our marriage may go sour and leave us emotionally numb. The demands of school may become too exasperating for us to handle. The pressures of our job may put us on edge. A newborn baby may take absolutely everything out of us. We can come to the place where we have no feelings left to keep us going. Or what we do have may become so frayed that we couldn't depend upon them for much of anything. If we are to survive spiritually at times like these, we must have something more than feelings to see us through.

LIVE BY FAITH, NOT FEELINGS

Now don't misunderstand. Becoming a Christian certainly doesn't mean that God expects us to abandon our feelings and become unemotional. He doesn't want us to become cold, calculating stoics. No! We are emotional beings; we have feelings. Feelings and emotions are part of our makeup. God made us that way. And there are many things in the Christian life about which we need to have deep feelings and express strong emotion. But nowhere does the Bible ever suggest that we should be led by our feelings or emotions. Instead, it says that we should "live by faith, not by sight" (2 Cor. 5:7). The Amplified New Testament expands on this idea when it says: "For we walk by faith [that is, we regulate our lives and conduct ourselves by our conviction or belief respecting man's relationship to God and divine things, with trust and holy fervor; thus we walk] not by sight or appearance." In other words, when we become Christians our lives should be ordered by the conviction that the teaching of Jesus develops within us, and not by our senses. We can no longer afford to let our feelings be our guide but we must see to it that they are safely guided by the Word of God. We must focus our attention on the truth of God's Word and follow it as our guiding star no matter how our feelings may try to manipulate us.

You will discover that when your faith starts acting upon God's Word, you will be stirred emotionally. Your feelings will be aroused – the appropriate kind: love, compassion, concern, enthusiasm, joy. And these feelings will complement your faith. But what you can't afford to do is get excited about excitement, emotional about emotion, and feel good about your feelings. To do this would take you nowhere. Your emotions must be subject to your faith at all times and be inspired by it.

FOLLOW JESUS' EXAMPLE

Biblical truth is always perfectly illustrated by Jesus. And he was filled with deep emotion. The same feelings you have he often experienced. He experienced compassion, deep concern, impatience, sorrow, and even at times anger. And since he was tempted in every way that we are, he was tempted to let his feelings dictate the course of his life and ministry. But he didn't allow his feelings to control him because he had an agenda for his life that had been determined by God. He had a divine purpose for being here. And he had solid convictions that determined his path. He came to do his Father's will and he would not permit anything or anyone to keep him from following it. He expressed deep feeling in doing his Father's will, but his emotions were always kept in check by his agenda. For example, he became very emotional as he considered going to the cross – so much so that blood issued from his sweat glands. But he gave himself up to the cross anyway because his convictions compelled him to. His stated purpose for coming into this world was "to give his life a ransom for many." And he did. He lived and died by his convictions.

That's how we must live! We must live by the agenda that God has set for us in his Word and has shown us in the life of Jesus. And whatever emotion that may stir within us needs to complement our faith.

We must continually live by faith's conviction if we are to walk in the steps of the Savior, because he will inevitably lead us to do things which will at first repulse our emotions. If we allow our feelings to control us, he will be very limited in his ability to lead us everywhere he wants to take us. So when he calls us into the altogether new, hard, and seemingly frightening things, it is then that we must "live by faith" – act on our convictions – because our feelings will say "no" to these new things.

We must understand that his desire to lead and direct our lives can never be fully realized as long as we allow our feelings to control us. They will say "no" to running the risk of failure or of being hurt or embarrassed. They will balk at the very thought of acknowledging wrong and confessing sin in our lives. They won't want to make apologies, restitution, or amends when called for. They won't want to abandon enmity, bitterness, and ill will when exposed. They won't want to forgive when there has been deep hurt. So if we allow ourselves to be controlled by our feelings we will probably never do many of the things our Christian conviction would compel us to do. That's why we must live by our convictions and not by our feelings.

It was conviction that compelled Jesus to go to the cross; it was conviction that led Paul to his death; it was conviction that led Jim Elliott and his companions to sacrifice their bodies to natives' spears as they attempted to win them to Christ. It will be conviction that will compel you to do every right and hard thing that your faith in Jesus will ever compel you to do.

Amy Grant captures all this in her song "Faith Walking People." She sings to God in the verse: "the secret of it all is trusting in You, and the wisdom You give." In the chorus she exhorts:

> Say goodbye to the feelings cause the feelings go away.
> Say goodbye to the people cause the people never stay.
> Say goodbye to the future if it blinds you to today.
> Say goodbye to the reasoning that's standing in the way.
> Oh we've got to break away
> Break away to be . . .
> Faith-walkin people can't rely on everything we feel.
> Faith-talkin people we must discern what's really real.
> Faith-walkin people can't believe in everything we see.
> Faith-talkin people seems like such a mystery.[1]

As Christians we don't do things because we feel like it but because truth demands it. So say goodbye to living by your feelings today and determine by God's grace and enabling to start living your new life in Christ by the counsel of God's Word and the example of the Lord Jesus. "Let us run with perseverance the race that is set before us, looking to Jesus the pioneer and perfecter of our faith . . ." (Heb. 12:1, 2).

---

[1]Written by Amy Grant and Brown Bannister, copyright 1979. Used by permission of Bug and Bear Music Company.

11 Becoming Doers of the Word

Getting believers to take action upon the Word of God has always posed a problem. It was certainly a problem that first century spiritual leaders grappled with. From Jesus to John, God's spokesmen were continually calling upon believers to translate God's word into life. Jesus issued the call a dozen different ways: "Not everyone who says to me, 'Lord, Lord,' will enter the kingdom of heaven, but only he who does the will of my Father who is in heaven"; "Everyone who hears these words of mine and puts them into practice is like a wise man" (Matt. 7:21, 24); "Someone told him, 'your mother and brothers are standing outside, wanting to speak to you.' He replied, 'Who is my mother, and who are my brothers? Whoever does the will of my Father in heaven is my brother and sister and mother'" (Matt. 12:47-50); "A woman in the crowd called out, 'Blessed is the mother who gave birth and nursed you.' He replied, 'Blessed rather are those who hear the Word of God and obey it'" (Luke 11:27, 28); "Once you know these things, you will be blessed if you do them" (John 13:17); "Why do you call me, 'Lord, Lord,' and do not do what I say?" (Luke 6:46). James reiterated the words of Jesus sometime later saying, "Do not merely listen to the word, and so deceive yourselves. Do what it says" (James 1:22). As the final inspired spokesman of the first century, John wrote, "let us not love with words of tongue but with actions and in truth" (1 John 3:18).

Things certainly haven't changed much. The problem of getting people to be doers of the Word still persists. James' call to "Do what it says" is as relevant and timely as it ever was. We modern believers like to think that our great need is one of hearing and knowing more of the Word, but it isn't. Most people already know far more than they ever put into practice. What more do we need to hear about pride, selfishness, discipline, love, faith, prayer, giving, service, or any other major matter before we begin doing something about them?

So let's give some serious attention to the matter of being doers of the Word and not mere hearers. Let's consider "Why We Are Called To Be Doers?", "What Hinders Our Becoming Doers?", "How Do We Become Doers?", "How Does Doing The Word Find Expression?", and finally, "What Will We Gain From Being Doers Of The Word?"

WHY ARE WE CALLED TO BE DOERS OF THE WORD?

Why are Christians called to be "doers of the Word" in the first place? Simply, because Christianity is meant to be a way of life and not just another religious ritual tacked on to it. The Word, therefore, becomes God's counsel and direction for how that life is to be lived out. If the Word is received only to be kept locked up in the mind and is not translated into life, Christianity becomes a matter of mere words. The Word remains mere word never to become the "word becomes flesh" in us. To fail to put the Word into practice is to relegate it to being mere theory. And though it may be absolute truth, it is at best only a good theory until it has been put into practice and has become the practical experience of the believer.

But the Word was not given to be just good theory – even the best. It was given to produce life. The words of God are the words of life. We sing that sometimes when we sing, "Sing them over again to me, Wonderful words of Life; Let me more of their beauty see, Wonderful words of Life . . ." Let us believe what we sing.

In James 1:23, James points out that anyone who fails to act upon the Word after having supposedly heard it, hasn't heard it in the first place. He is "like the man who looks at his face in the mirror and, after looking at himself, goes away and immediately forgets what he looks like."

WHAT HINDERS OUR BECOMING DOERS OF THE WORD?

If our problem is not one of needing to hear more or know more about the Word but one of doing it, what hinders us in this? What keeps us from being "doers of the word?" A number of things do. Let's consider some of them.

For one thing, we hear the Word and don't act upon it immediately. For example, we'll read something from scripture or hear a message in the church assembly and become stirred and inspired, but we don't act upon it immediately. Monday starts a new work week; we get busy in its activities and we don't act upon what we've heard all week. Another week rolls around and we hear more but still don't act upon it. And so it goes, the more we hear the less we do until our much hearing and little doing harden us to the truth. And so we become experts in criticism and evasion of the truth. We become just like the Pharisees we despise; we become experts in the truth, but we do not practice it.

Another reason today's believers do more "hearing" than "doing" is because there is little or no accountability within the church to compel them to do otherwise. Members are held accountable to no one for whether they are or are not doers of the Word or whether they take action on some of it or all of it. It's all left up to them. The Word is taught and the individual decides what he will or will not act upon. More often than not, his choice is very much like his choice of food at a cafeteria. He picks and chooses what suits him. And that usually amounts to a pie, cake or ice cream diet. Not hardly the kind that produces good health and strength. But who is there to tell him to "eat his spinach?"

The "cafeteria" approach to the Word has, as you would expect, led many to conclude: "If I don't have a conviction in a given area I feel no compulsion or responsibility to act." And so they don't. And many things that the Word calls for are never acted upon.

At times, some excuse themselves from doing some of the things that the Word calls for with the explanation: "I don't see the logic or reason in doing what it says." But, of course, if we did, why would we need God or his Word to counsel us in the first place? We would be perfectly capable of successfully directing our own lives.

Sometimes someone will excuse himself from following the Word by explaining, "Others aren't doing it, why should I?"

Many are fully satisfied in having their religious emotions placated through merely hearing the Word. They listen for the sheer pleasure of listening. It's a pleasure closely related to that which one gets from the theater or the movies or T.V. These people delight in having the teacher or preacher play the piano with their emotions. If in one session he can make them laugh, cry, become excited, experience joy, be serious, feel guilty – run the gauntlet of emotional experience – it has been a great session. And the experience in itself becomes satisfaction enough. There is no need to consider doing the Word.

Not too few consider the Word as an object of intellectual stimulus and speculation. It has within it exciting and stimulating concepts to be explored, discussed, debated, and argued about as in the manner of the Athenians (Acts 17:21). These spend "their time doing nothing but talking about and listening" to the Word. But this should be understandable, since our western educational system has been patterned after the Greek model rather than the Hebrew. Educationally speaking, in and out of the church we have been Hellenized instead of evangelized. We have been taught for the sake of teaching rather than for the purpose of learning how to live. As the new "Israel of God" we need to return to the education philosophy of our spiritual ancestors who taught to produce life and sought to be an embodiment of their teaching.

Closely related to this, the Word is for others, great doctrine. They get caught up in doctrinal issues. They spend their time researching prophecy and having prophetic conferences. They occupy themselves with the details of Christ's second coming forgetting that Jesus said, "Occupy till I come" (Luke 19:13 KJV), not "Be occupied with my coming."

To get to the bottom line on why most of us do more hearing of the word than doing: it is due to disobedience and unbelief. We are just blatantly disobedient. God knew that would be a big problem common to most of us and that is why He continually calls us to obedience.

Unbelief is our second basic problem. Jesus pinpointed most of us when in Matthew 6:30 he said, "O you of little faith." In Hebrews chapters three and four the problem is further highlighted. Our problem of unbelief is threefold: we don't believe the Word is the Word of God – if we did there would be no question about its reliability; we don't believe the Word is the Word of truth – if we did there would be no hesitancy in our acting upon it; we don't truly believe that Jesus is Lord – if we did we would do what he says because his Lordship over us is demonstrated in our doing what he says. (Cf. Luke 6:46).

HOW TO BECOME DOERS OF THE WORD

Having considered some of the things that hinder us from being "doers of the Word," perhaps we are now better able to determine what course we should take in order to become doers of it. It would seem obvious that one thing that we need to do is to repent of those things that we have allowed to hinder us from taking action upon what the word calls for. We need to abandon our unbelief, disobedience, spectatoring, picking and choosing what we like, getting our emotional, intellectual, and doctrinal kicks from merely hearing, and anything else that has been keeping us from being a doer of the Word. This needs to be followed by a decision of commitment or re-commitment to the Lordship of Christ and to doing what he says. Too many of us have spent too much of our lives as believers doing everything with the Word except the one thing needful – doing it; putting it into practice. Let us resolve this very day to spend the rest of our Christian lives putting the Word of God into practice in our daily lives.

HOW WILL DOING THE WORD FIND EXPRESSION?

How will determining to become a "doer of the word" find practical expression in our daily lives? Both James and John give us some direction. James chooses two examples of extreme human need in his day to teach us that living out the Word of God will mean ministering to those who are in need.

He says, "Religion ('worship' would be a better word for the Greek word used, for *threskea* refers to the outward expression of worship) that God our Father accepts as pure and faultless is this: to look after orphans and widows in their distress and to keep oneself from being polluted by the world" (James 1:27). In James' day there were no orphanages to care for those who were left without parents. There was no "North Shore Orphanage" in Galilee or "Inner City Orphanage" in Jerusalem. Orphans were left to fend for themselves or die; unless, of course, someone wanted to raise them for prostitution or slave labor. Widows usually had two choices for survival: sell themselves into slavery or become prostitutes.

The world was "a corrupt generation," it was "crooked and depraved," it was an "evil age" which was "under the control of the evil one" (Acts 2:40; Phil. 2:15; Gal. 1:4; 1 John 5:19). It was a contaminate to avoid at all costs. God's Word was given to act as an anti-pollutant. Its application to life leads to purity.

John, like James, teaches that living out the Word will involve us in seeking to meet the needs of others. He writes, "If anyone has material possessions and sees his brother in need but has no pity on him, how can the love of God be in him?" He goes on to say, "let us not love with words or tongue but with actions and in truth" (1 John 3:17, 18).

WHAT DO WE GAIN FROM BEING DOERS?

And finally, what do we gain if we become "doers of the Word" and not mere hearers? Much in every way. But perhaps James sums it up best when he says, "the man who looks intently into the perfect law that gives freedom, and continues to do this, not forgetting what he has heard, but *doing* it – he will be *blessed* in what he does" (1:25). Doers of the Word enter into the blessed life. What greater reward than that!

12 What On Earth Are You Doing For Heaven's Sake?

Too many people both in and out of the church believe that Christianity is just another moral philosophy concerned with ridding the individual of his fleshly, passionate sins and checking further indulgence. Surely you've heard this philosophy; maybe you've advocated it yourself. It usually goes something like this: "I don't do anyone any harm. I don't drink, I don't carouse around, I'm not a thief, etc."

This is a negative goodness. It may not involve any goodness at all. It may be simply cutting down on one's badness.

THE FUTILITY OF NEGATIVE GOODNESS

A person could cease from indulging some of his appetites and passions without being a disciple of Jesus at all. The Pharisees were experts at negative morality and yet they contrived to eliminate the greatest witness to goodness the world has ever known.

It is possible to profess a negative goodness while all the world around stumbles in darkness toward an eventual hell. Witnessing to one's curbed appetites is no gospel. In fact, it can be an expression of egoism. It can be the smug, complacent witness to one's pride of achievement. It can be the repetition of the Pharisee (Luke 18) who prayed, "God, I thank you that I'm not like other men . . . ."

When offered in any area other than religion, the argument of the negative becomes ridiculous. Try it, for example, on patriotism: "I don't burn the flag, I don't cheat on my income tax, I'm not trying to evade paying my property taxes, I'm not plotting to overthrow the government, etc." The question soon arises, "Now that we've learned all that you *don't* do, what *do* you do to demonstrate your patriotism?"

Better yet, try it on marriage. Your wife gets up early with you and fixes your breakfast. Later she gets the children up and dresses and feeds them. Besides caring for them all day she puts out the washing, finishes up her ironing from the last wash, straightens up the house, cooks two more meals and does the dishes; and, as she comes in from mowing the lawn and washing the car, she plops down in the chair opposite you. You're stretched out in your favorite chair in front of the T.V. with your feet on the ottoman sipping a tall cold beverage. During a commercial you turn your attention from your T.V. program to her and say: "You know, you're a lucky girl to be married to a guy like me. I don't smoke, I don't drink, I don't swear, I don't beat you and the kids, I don't carouse around or spend every night out with the boys . . . ."

About that time she interrupts confirmingly with, "No, all you do is lie here in front of this stupid television!" This is her sarcastic way of saying, "Now that I know all that you don't do, which serves to make you a good husband, may I inquire about what you *do* do?"

The same question must be asked of those whose profession of discipleship is a negative goodness: "What on earth are you doing for heaven's sake? So you refrain from indulging some of your passions and desires. What positive good are you doing anyone?" Discipleship doesn't mean merely, "Knock off the sin!" It means that, yes; but even more it means, "Get busy for righteousness sake!"

INACTIVITY IS SIN

One of the Bible's main definitions of sin equates sin with failure to act upon what we know is right to do: "Whoever knows what is right to do and fails to do it, for him it is sin" (James 4:17).

The big sin in the life of most disciples is not so much that of indulging appetites and passions as it is failure to take positive action on what they know they ought to do. It is the sin of omission. Too many are living in known sin and need to repent, and the known sins are not those so often cited by the moral reformers. Rather, they are the sins of omission.

Maybe the reason why more prayers are not being answered, why the Lord is not a power within, and why there is too little victorious life in modern disciples, is that too many disciples need to repent of the sins of omission.

OMITTED GOOD INVITES DISASTER

In the parables of Jesus that deal with the end and with judgment, what do you suppose are the sins that condemn? Idolatry? Adultery? Impurity? No – the sins of *omission*. In every case the sin is an omitted good.

In the parable of the rich fool (Luke 12), the man stands condemned because he was "not rich toward God." He didn't do anyone any harm. He just didn't do anyone any good. His sin was one of *omission*.

In the parable of the fig tree (Luke 13), the tree is ordered destroyed because it has borne no fruit. The good has not been forthcoming.

In the parable of the rich man and Lazarus (Luke 16), the rich man didn't feed the beggar. No sins of commission are cited. It is just that the good had been *omitted*.

In both the parables of the talents and the pounds (Matthew 25; Luke 19), condemnation came to the servant who failed to utilize his gift. He isn't cited for blatant acts of commission but for what he *omitted*.

And finally, in the scene of the last judgment (Matthew 25), the goats are separated from the sheep and placed on the left hand in condemnation for what they didn't do! The King said, "I was hungry and you gave me no food (*omission*), I was thirsty and you gave me no drink (*omission*), I was a stranger and you did not welcome me (*omission*), naked and you did not clothe me (*omission*), sick and in prison and you did not visit me (*omission*)."

What receives condemnation in Christ's eyes is not doing the good we can, the good we ought, the good that he himself has exemplified for us.

DISCIPLESHIP DEMONSTRATED

Discipleship means more than refraining from evil or talking about good. It means a positive demonstration of good. It means "doing the Word," "bearing much fruit," "working," "serving," "giving," "loving." The kingdom is more than just philosophizing; it is "righteousness, and peace, and joy in the Holy Spirit." It consists not in talk but in power (Rom. 14:17; 1 Cor. 4:20). The faith that follows Jesus is of necessity an active, working, producing faith; or it is no faith at all. It is as James puts it, "So faith by itself if it has no works, is dead" (James 2:17).

No one can say, "I belong to Jesus," without to some degree doing as he did and walking in the same way in which he walked (1 John 2:6). And Peter characterizes him as one who "went about doing good" (Acts 10:38).

It is not enough to say, "I don't do . . . ." The big question is, "What do you do? What on earth are you doing for heaven's sake?"

It is only as our lives are filled with positive goodness that sin is really eliminated from life. To merely cease from destructive sins and habits is to create a vacuum which invites multiplied evil (see Luke 11:24-26).

13 Saved to Serve

It is very important to know that becoming a Christian means that you must abandon the obsessions of your past to serve the true and living God. Paul describes our conversion as a turning "to God from idols to *serve* the living and true God" (1 Thess. 1:9). The writer of Hebrews says that it is a cleansing of "our consciousness from acts that lead to death, so that we may serve the living God!" (Heb. 9:14). Paul tells us in Ephesians that we have been saved by grace through faith and have been "created in Christ Jesus to do good works, which God prepared in advance for us to do" (Eph. 2:10). In Titus he teaches us that the purpose of Jesus' coming and giving himself for us on the cross was so "that he might redeem us from every lawless deed and purify for himself his own special people, zealous for good works" (Titus 2:14 NKJV). In Romans he says to us, "my brothers, you also died to the law through the body of Christ, that you might belong to another, to him who was raised from the dead, in order that we might bear fruit to God" (Rom. 7:4).

As you can see, the subject of Christian service is not a one-passage subject. This sampling of scripture should serve to make it clear that God has created us to be servants and wants us to spend our lives doing what pleases and glorifies him. Now that you have become a Christian you can no longer consider your life to be yours to do with as you please. You no longer belong to yourself. You have been "bought at a price" and should "therefore honor God with" your life (1 Cor. 6:19, 20). Jesus purchased you by his death on the cross and therefore you "should live no longer for" yourself, "but for him who died for" you and made you his own (2 Cor. 5:15). You have been saved to serve our Lord Jesus Christ.

THE EMPHASIS ON SERVICE

The repeated emphasis of the biblical message to believers is that they have been called to serve Christ through their good works. We will never be so much like our Lord Jesus as when we are doing this. He told us that his reason for coming was to serve. In the Gospel of Mark, he said, "the Son of Man did not come to be served, but to serve, and to give his life as a ransom for many" (Mark 10:45). In the Gospel of Luke he said, "I am among you as one who serves" (Luke 22:27). In Acts, Peter described him as one who "went around doing good" (Acts 10:38).

One of the main things the Apostles prayed for when praying for believers was for them to be servants. Paul prayed that the Philippian Christians would be "filled with the fruit of righteousness that comes through Jesus Christ" (Phil. 1:11). He prayed that the Colossians would "bear fruit in every good work" (Col. 1:10). And he prayed that the Thessalonians would be encouraged and strengthened "in every good deed and word" (2 Thess. 2:17).

The reason God gave us his Word was "so that the man of God may be thoroughly equipped for every good work" (2 Tim. 3:16, 17) and serve God effectively and fruitfully.

The reason God gives spiritual gifts to believers is to equip them to be more effective in serving. The Apostle Peter says, "Each one should use whatever spiritual gift he has received to serve others, faithfully administering God's grace in its various forms" (1 Pet. 4:10).

The reason God provides the church with leadership is "to prepare God's people for works of service" (Eph. 4:12).

Christians are called to assemble regularly for the purpose of considering how they might "spur one another on toward love and good deeds" (Heb. 10:24).

Good works are what will serve to silence unbelieving critics and actually lead them to glorify God. Peter exhorts believers, "Live such good lives among the pagans that, though they accuse you of doing wrong, they may see your good deeds and glorify God on the day he visits us" (1 Pet. 2:12).

In five out of the seven letters Jesus addressed to the seven churches of Asia in chapters two and three of Revelation he began with, "I know your deeds" (Rev. 2:2, 19; 3:1, 8, 15). The service of believers was obviously a matter of prime importance to Jesus.

Jesus went so far as to say that good works would serve as the proof of genuine discipleship. He said, "By this my Father is glorified, that you bear much fruit, and so prove to be my disciples" (John 15:8, RSV). In the judgment scene of Matthew 25, he equated saving faith with service to those in need and said that without it no one would enter the eternal kingdom. James added, "faith by itself, if it is not accompanied by action, is dead" (James 2:17).

Though we are not saved *by* good works, we are certainly saved *for* them and they will witness that we have come to saving faith. There is a sense in which it could be said that a person has not fully accepted the call of Christ upon his life until he has begun a life of serving.

SERVICE: THE WAY TO GREATNESS

Jesus repeatedly repudiated the world's concept of greatness and taught that the serving life is the way to be great. On one occasion the disciples of Jesus were wrangling over positions of authority in his kingdom. He called them together and said,

> You know that the rulers of the Gentiles lord it over them, and their high officials exercise authority over them. Not so with you. Instead, whoever wants to become great among you must be your servant, and whoever wants to be first must be your slave – just as the Son of Man did not

> come to be served, but to serve, and to give his life a ransom for many (Matt. 20:25-28).

The importance that Jesus attached to this principle is emphasized by the number of times he repeated it. He said to the Pharisees, "The greatest among you will be your servant. For whoever exalts himself will be humbled, and whoever humbles himself will be exalted" (Matt. 23:11, 12). When the disciples were arguing again about who was the greatest he told them, "If anyone wants to be first, he must be the very last, and the servant of all" (Mark 9:35). When the disciples were disputing about greatness at the Last Supper he said to them, "The kings of the Gentiles lord it over them, and those who exercise authority over them are given the title Benefactor. But you are not to be like that. Instead, the greatest among you should be like the youngest, and the one who rules like the one who serves" (Luke 22:25, 26).

Though the world still believes that greatness is equated with standing above others in fame, fortune, and power and in being able to have control over them, both time and life itself have proven that Jesus taught the way of true greatness when he called us to be servants of all. Those who have heeded his call have proven to be history's truly great ones.

SERVICE: THE WAY TO BLESSEDNESS

The way to a blessed, fulfilling life as a Christian is to give yourself in service to Christ. Jesus said, "It is more blessed to give than to receive" (Acts 20:35). He illustrated this principle in what he said to a prominent spiritual leader of his day: "When you give a luncheon or dinner, do not invite your friends, your brothers or relatives, or your rich neighbors; if you do, they may invite you back and so you will be repaid. But when you give a banquet, invite the poor, the crippled, the lame, the blind, and you will be blessed" (Luke 14:12-14).

As you start serving you will begin to discover that serving Christians are joyful Christians. In serving you will enter into a dimension of fellowship with Jesus that can be experienced in no other way. And that will bring you an increased sense of joy and fulfillment and will accelerate your growth and maturity.

HOW SHALL I SERVE?

Assuming that you have become convinced that the serving life is the fulfilling life, you will surely want to know how to get started.

Jesus is always the supreme example for the Christian in whatever he is called to do. And he is certainly the example of a servant. So he can best show the way. Do you remember Peter saying that Jesus "went around doing good?" Let's consider some of the things he went around doing.

His ministry is described in his own words as one where he preached "good news to the poor," proclaimed "freedom for the prisoners and recovery of sight to the blind," and "release" for the oppressed (Luke 4:18). In other words, he taught, healed, counseled, comforted, defended, and rescued people. He sought to bring love, mercy, and justice to the poor. He sought to bring an end to tyranny and oppression for all who were enslaved in any way. And he sought to right the wrongs of the oppressed and protect the defenseless against the misuse of power. He was always giving himself in service to others.

If you want to live and serve "as Jesus did" (1 John 2:6), these are some of the things that you will want to consider. Now, of course, much of your service will of necessity be done in concert with other believers because as a member of Christ's church you are bonded to them in fellowship, certainly the fellowship of service.

God has given every believer at least one spiritual gift with which to serve (1 Cor. 7:7) and that gift is given to be used for the common good of the church (1 Cor. 12:7; 1

Pet. 4:10). "We have different gifts, according to the grace given us," Paul says (Rom. 12:6), and these gifts are to be used within the church to strengthen and equip it so that it in turn can effectively minister to the world.

The basic serving gifts are seven in number and are listed in Romans 12:6-8. They are: prophesy (proclaiming the Word), serving, teaching (explaining the Word), encouraging, giving, leading, and showing mercy. You will in time discover that you have one of these gifts and that you will be able to serve best in the area in which you are gifted. You will also find out that service offered in this area can be done with a maximum of effectiveness and a minimum of effort.

How can you discover what your gift is? Here are a few simple suggestions. Ask God to reveal it to you. Experiment by taking advantage of whatever opportunities you are given to serve. Note what you like to do and what you do well. Ask fellow Christians to give you their evaluation of what you do well. And note what you feel compelled by God to do.

A WARNING

Here is a final warning to those who would hesitate to get involved in service: it is a principle of scripture that uselessness invites disaster. Jesus repeatedly warned of the consequence of not becoming involved in serving. He said, "Not everyone who says to me, 'Lord, Lord,' will enter the kingdom of heaven" (Matt. 7:21). He followed this statement with the parable of the wise and foolish builders and said this about the foolish builder: "The one who hears my words and does not put them into practice is like a man who built a house on the ground without a foundation. The moment the torrent struck that house, it collapsed and its destruction was complete" (Luke 6:49). In the parable of the fig tree he told of a man that had been looking for fruit on his fig tree for three years and had found none. "Cut it down," he said. "Why should it use up the soil?" The caretaker of the garden entreated him to spare it for one more year while he dug around it and fertilized it. He replied, "If it bears fruit next year, fine! If not, then cut it down" (Luke 13:6-9). In the parable of the talents in Matthew 25, the man who was entrusted with one talent by his master but did not put it to use was rebuked, stripped of his talent, and punished. The parable of the ten minas in Luke 19 is a twin parable to the parable of the talents and draws the same conclusion. In the similitude of the vine and the branches in John 15:1-8 where Jesus said, "I am the vine; you (disciples) are the branches," "and my Father is the gardener," he adds, "He (the Father) cuts off every branch in me that bears no fruit." In the judgment scene in Matthew 25 Jesus is pictured commending and rewarding those who have exercised their faith in service, and condemning to "eternal punishment" those who haven't.

FINAL WORD

The charge that Paul gave to the Corinthian Christians near the end of his first letter to them could serve as a lifelong exhortation to service: "Therefore, my beloved brethren, be steadfast, immovable, always abounding in the work of the Lord, knowing that in the Lord your labor is not in vain" (1 Cor. 15:58).

14 How Much Shall I Give?

The response of everyone who becomes a Christian and is blessed with the gift of God's grace is usually to begin sharing their income with the Lord. It is not uncommon to see one rise from the baptismal waters and immediately offer a gift to the Lord. New converts are always wanting to know how they may obtain a set of offering envelopes.

When it comes to giving to the Lord, the big question is not "shall I give" but rather how *much* shall I give? Is my giving left to my own discretion or has God specified how much I should give?" The answer is both "yes" and "no." No, it is not left up to us to determine the minimum amount that we should give. That has been determined by the Lord himself. But yes, we can make the decision determining the maximum amount that we may give. "What then should be the starting minimum in my giving?" The Bible never speaks of anything less than a *tithe*.

WHAT IS A TITHE?

If the Bible speaks of our minimum giving in terms of a tithe, what then is meant by this term? First of all, let us consider what it is not. "Tithe" could never apply to any gift representing less than one tenth of one's income. For the word "tithe" comes from the Hebrew word *Asar* which literally means "tenth." Tithe means "a tenth of the increase." In Leviticus 27:30 God said, "All the tithe of the land, whether of the seed of the land or of the fruit of the trees, is the Lord's; it is holy to the Lord." To tithe is to give one tenth of one's increase to the Lord.

IS TITHING A CHRISTIAN PRACTICE?

Some have objected to tithing saying that it belongs to the "law" of the Old Testament and that we Christians are not under law but under "grace" and our law is "love." But though we are under grace and our law is love it is not true that tithing belongs exclusively to the "law" of the Old Testament. Tithing was practiced by God's people for over a thousand years before the law was ever instituted. In Genesis 14:20 you can read where Abram practiced tithing: "And Abram gave him (Melchizedek) a tenth of everything." In Genesis 28:22 you can read where Jacob in an expression of commitment to God promised to tithe: "and of all that you give me I will give you a tenth."

Tithing, like some other common practices of God's people of old, was incorporated into the law when it was finally instituted because it was simply God's immutable truth. It was not part of the ceremonial law which ended with Christ. Nor was it symbolical or figurative of something to come. When the reasons which originate a law continue to exist and there is not plain repeal of the law, the law remains in force. The tithe, therefore, passes right into the Christian era and New Testament scripture advocates it. (Read Matt. 5:17-20; 23:23; 1 Cor. 9:7-14).

The only freedom that the Christian has in his giving is to give more than the tithe. To give less is to give less than God has decreed. To give less is to say that Jews who lived under law were more generous in their giving to God than are Christians who live under grace. Isn't grace more demanding than law? And should it not outdo whatever law calls for?

WHO SHOULD TITHE?

Who should tithe? Every person who professes to be a child of God who has any kind of income, whether it be a young person receiving an allowance or a worker receiving wages for his labor. Parents should teach their believing children that giving at least a tenth of whatever money they make to the Lord is a part of their Christian worship.

FOR WHAT PURPOSE ARE TITHES AND OFFERINGS GIVEN?

Tithes and offerings are given for four main purposes:

1. *To acknowledge God's ownership of all things and that it is by his power that we get wealth.* It is in recognition of this that we give him "the rent" of the tithe. "The earth is the Lord's and everything in it, the world and all who live in it" (Ps. 24:1). "You shall remember the Lord your God, for it is he who gives you the power to get wealth" (Deut. 8:18).
2. *The tithe was instituted as a means of perpetuating the Kingdom of God.* Read 1 Corinthians 9:13, 14 and you will see that just as the tithe was the means of supporting the ministry of the Old Testament period so it is meant to be the means of supporting the ministry of the New Testament era.
3. *Tithing acknowledges one's obedience to God's will.* "Under the test of this service (giving), you will glorify God by your obedience" (2 Cor. 9:13).
4. *In tithing one acknowledges his personal receipt of the gospel of Christ and the salvation of his soul.* "Under the test of this service, you will glorify God by your obedience in acknowledging the gospel of Christ" (2 Cor. 9:13).

WHAT IF I CAN'T AFFORD TO TITHE?

Some may object, "I can't afford to give a tenth of my income to the Lord." My dear Christian friend, you cannot afford *not* to tithe, because to fail to do so witnesses a lack of faith and obedience; and possible selfishness and covetousness on your part. And it involves you in telling the God of the Universe what you would not dare tell your government when it asks you for twice as much.

If you say, "I just don't have sufficient income to give a tithe to the Lord," then you need to remember that the people of God of both the Old and New Testament periods who practiced tithing faithfully were some of the poorest people history has known. If you say, "I just can't squeeze a tithe into our budget" – how do you know whether you can or not if you have never tried? God calls upon us to do this as an act of faith and as an expression of our obedience. If we have to figure out how it's all going to work out, then it's no longer an act of faith. It's merely an expression of human ingenuity which excludes God from being an active part in the whole matter.

You may say, "That's asking too much! I work hard for my money and it's mine to do with as I choose. It's mine to spend on my family, to pay my bills, to buy things that I want." It's true that God gives you most of what you earn to do these things. But he says that at least a tithe belongs to him. He gives us the resources and the power and ability to work those resources to get everything that we have, and he asks for at least a tenth of it in return to acknowledge that it all comes from him, and that we are dependent upon him.

To fail to give God at least a tithe of one's income is to live as a thief, and the Bible doesn't hesitate to say so. In Malachi 3:8, 9 God asks, "Will man rob God? Yet you are robbing me. But you say, 'How are we robbing you?' In your tithes and offerings. You are cursed with a curse, for you are robbing me." He goes on to command in verse 10: "Bring the whole tithe into the storehouse." It is doubtful that any Christian would think of stealing from the local grocery or department store, for that would be considered sin. And if that be so, how much greater a sin it would be to steal from God. And that is precisely what God says his people are doing when they take any part of the tithe and spend it on themselves. They are stealing from him. They might just as well come up and take a handful of money out of the offering plate at the close of a worship hour and put it in their pocket and go out and spend it on Sunday dinner for the family.

The Lord knows what everyone is giving or failing to give to him. He watches the offering plate every time it's passed. He certainly did when he was with us in the flesh. "And he sat down opposite the treasury and watched the multitude putting money into the treasury" (Mark 12:41). The Lord is present in every assembly of the church observing everything that goes on. He sees the gifts of grateful hearts who respond in obedience by giving a tithe or more. And he takes note of those who give less than they know they should, and is fully aware of their reasoning for doing such.

THE BLESSING OF TITHING

Giving a tenth of one's income to the Lord is by no means meant to be a drudgery nor will it result in hardship. To the contrary. It will result in blessings so great that the believer will not be able to contain them all. This is the promise of God's Word. Look again at Malachi 3:10: "Bring the full tithe into the storehouse that there may be food in my house; and thereby put me to the test says the Lord of hosts, if I will not open the windows of heaven for you and pour down for you an *overflowing blessing*." Hear Jesus promise, "Give, and it will be given to you, a good measure, pressed down, shaken together and running over, will be the measure you get back" (Luke 6:38). Listen to 2 Corinthians 9:6: "Whoever sows sparingly will also reap sparingly, and whoever sows generously will also reap generously." Listen again to 2 Corinthians 9:10-11: "He who supplies seed to the sower and bread for food will supply and multiply your resources and *increase* the harvest of your righteousness. You will be *enriched* in every *way* for great generosity . . . ." How many there are who will testify to this truth. Consider the testimony of a fairly new Christian which is typical: "You just can't outgive God! Every time I increase my giving, the Lord blesses me with multiplied increased blessings." When you make a decision to be faithful to God in giving him what you know he would have you give, peace will flood your heart with the knowledge that you have acted in obedience to His will.

START TITHING TODAY!

If as a child of God you have not started tithing yet, in the name of the Lord Jesus will you not start today! Will you not start giving at least one tenth of your income to God? Perhaps you could and should give more. And do not give a tenth of what is left after all the deductions have been taken from your paycheck, but give a tenth of what you actually earn. Put God to the test as Malachi 3:10 calls upon you to do, and see if your life does not become one flooded with blessings from above. Exercise your faith in this matter of giving. Surrender in obedience to the will of God in your giving and remember this: the main reason God wants at least a tenth of your income is so that he may have *you.* He knows that "where your treasure is, there will your heart be also," as Jesus said it would be in Matthew 6:21. And he knows it would take at least a tenth of our income to get our hearts. And second, he wants to demonstrate that he can take our nine tenths and bless it to become more than what those have who in unbelief give little or nothing.

God gave his all to save us from our sin and make us his children forever. Can we respond to his generosity with anything less than what he calls for from us?

15 Twelve Guidelines For Christian Living

One of the ways we can grow as Christians is to learn from the accumulated wisdom of older believers or those who have passed on before us. Their experience of living many years as Christians should have enabled them to learn invaluable lessons from which we could profit much. Those who have been around for some time have seen the emergence of a few life-guiding principles that would be invaluable for any young Christian to have in their possession. Let's consider twelve that have proven to have lasting value.

1. *To the degree that you are prepared, to that degree you can be used in the service of the Lord.*

Many, though they be blessed with innate talent and ability, are limited in their service due to their lack of preparation. Doors simply do not open to those who are not prepared to pass through them.

God, it would seem, has always placed a premium upon preparedness. Moses and David, outstanding leaders of the Old Testament, were men of much preparation. Before leading the children of Israel out of Egyptian bondage to freedom, Moses was schooled for eighty years for the job. He spent forty years in training in the courts of Egypt and forty years serving as a shepherd in Midian. David spent forty years in preparation as both shepherd and warrior before becoming Israel's greatest king.

Never let it be said that the apostles of the New Testament were ignorant, ill-prepared men. Three years of constant companionship with Jesus gave them a better education than any have ever had. And Paul's credentials would certainly satisfy anyone's qualifications.

The better prepared you become the better equipped you will be to serve. And you will find more areas of service opening up to you. Those who usually complain over lack of opportunity to serve and be used are usually those lacking in preparation.

2. *It is necessary not only to know God, but also to know man.*

If our main work as disciples of Jesus is to introduce men to God, we not only need to know God but we also need to know man if we are to introduce them to each other. If we become knowledgeable of one to the neglect of the other, we cannot be effective in making the introduction. If we know only God we risk being "too heavenly minded to be of any earthly good." If we know only man we are apt to be "too earthbound to be of any heavenly good."

We need not only to be students of the Scriptures in pursuit of a knowledge of God, but we likewise need to be students of humanity.

3. *Ninety-five percent of all the problems in the church are "people problems."*

So often the problems in the church are said to be impersonal ones. When there is division among brethren the reasons usually given are differing theological viewpoints, doctrinal differences, or procedural disagreement. Seldom, if ever, does anyone admit that a problem exists because of differences they have with others. And yet, if you were to get to the bottom you would find that about ninety-five percent of the time the problems were "people problems." Two people can't get along. They are jealous or resentful of each other. They feel that they have been slighted. But rather than admitting to this as the problem, facing it squarely, and settling it, the usual procedure is to hide behind the facade of the impersonal and let the problem smolder.

4. *One must constantly seek to have a sense of what is vital.*

It is so easy to get sidetracked from what is really important and give yourself to that which is secondary and unimportant. Paul must have realized how easily this could happen for he prayed for the Philippians (1:10, *ANT*), "that you may surely learn to sense what is vital, and approve and prize what is excellent and of real value." "What is vital?", you may ask. Paul said that which was of "first importance" as revealed to him was the gospel of Jesus Christ (1 Cor. 15:3, 4), and that he had "decided to know nothing among you except Jesus Christ and him Crucified" (1 Cor. 2:2). We must continually guard against letting anything or anyone replace Jesus as the object of our loyalty and affections. Jesus alone is vital! Have a continual, growing sense and awareness of him. Have a sense of what is vital only as it centers in and relates to him.

5. *You cannot live on yesterday's manna or experiences – study!*

What a temptation it is to rest in the truth learned yesterday and reminisce over past experience. But to live in the past, no matter how great the truth or exhilarating the experience, is to have our spiritual growth seriously impeded. We need to thank God for all truth we've already received and for the great experiences he's blessed us with, for we can build upon them. But we must "press on toward the goal for the prize of the upward call of God in Christ Jesus" (Phil. 3:14). If we have gathered up some significant truths, well and good, but there is so much more truth in Jesus yet to discover! If we have experienced something of Christ and the new life in him, how wonderful, but there is so much more of him yet to experience! Study! "Grow in the grace and knowledge of our Lord and Savior Jesus Christ" (2 Pet. 3:18).

6. *No one is blessed with every gift that God can bestow. One must discover his gift or gifts and concentrate on effectively utilizing them.*

Every Christian has been blessed with at least one spiritual gift (Rom. 12:4-8). Some may have been given several. But no one has been given all of them, although sometimes it almost seems that way. It is both futile and frustrating for any individual to attempt to do everything that members of the church are called upon to do. Wise and fruitful is the person who discovers the particular gift God has assigned him (1 Cor. 12:11; Heb. 2:4) and concentrates upon using it. Undoubtedly, each will make his discovery in his own way. It can begin with a concerned seeking accompanied by a prayerful request for God's assistance. Usually one will find it to be something that he can do well and enjoys doing. When the discovery is finally made, one needs to concentrate the effort of his labor in his defined field of endeavor and leave the rest of the work of the Kingdom to those who are gifted in other areas.

7. *Remember, you are not God. Leave something for him to do.*

It is quite easy for a concerned Christian to become a practicing atheist. This happens when one comes to believe that nothing in the Kingdom will succeed unless it has his personal attention. Souls cannot be saved unless *he* witnesses to them. Problems cannot be solved unless *his* counsel is sought. Plans cannot be developed without *his* inspiration. And so the compulsion to be the stimulating factor in everything can rule God out. But it's disastrous to eliminate God. It takes its toll on anyone who tries it. He soon wears himself out, worries himself sick, and erodes family relationships due to neglect, to say the least.

Certainly, everyone needs to be a concerned, zealous worker for the Lord. But they need to recognize the limitations of their humanity and commit to the Lord all that they cannot do, convinced that his concern and ability is far greater than theirs.

8. *Cast all your anxieties on him, else you will go mad!*

To live as a Christian, particularly as one intimately involved in the inner workings of a local congregation, is to be confronted with many anxiety producing people and problems. The Lord never promised that becoming a Christian would exempt us from problems. Often it serves to multiply them. If you allow yourself to become the depository of every problem that comes along, the accumulated weight and anxiety will in time rob you of your sanity. The prescription "Cast all your anxieties on him, for he cares about you" (1 Pet. 5:7) has helped many a faithful servant maintain mental health. The sooner we learn to transfer the cares and anxieties of the day to God the sooner we will learn to live in peace.

9. *Never forget that the church belongs to Christ. He alone is its head.*

In our possessiveness there may be times when we tend to forget this and think of the church as ours to do with as we will. No, it is his. And, since he is its head, we need to constantly seek his counsel in all that we do. The church can well do without its Diotrephes (3 John 9); they have done enough hurt already. If we would desire to rise to prominence let us do so as our Lord directed: "whoever would be great among you must be your servant, and whoever would be first among you must be slave of all" (Mark 10:43, 44).

10. *Do not be hasty in the making of important decisions. Do not operate on emotional impulse.*

How many are still living in regret over some important decision made in an impulsive moment of anger or desire. How they dearly wish that they would have shelved their decision for a period of thought and prayer. It was a wise professor, indeed, who advised his young ministerial students: "When in the course of your ministry, there come those times when you conclude, 'I've had it! I'm going to turn in my resignation!', go ahead, write it out. But then put it in your desk drawer for at least a week. Afterwards, take it out, read it, and then see if that's what you still want to do."

As Christians, we are directed not to live by emotional impulse, but by faith. Paul wrote, "we walk by faith, not by sight" (2 Cor. 5:7). If we allow ourselves to be directed by our faith and not our feelings, it is doubtful that there will ever be much of anything for which there will be regret.

11. *Remember who you are at all times, to whom you belong, and who it is that is in you.*

You are a son of God. God is your Father. You are a joint-heir with Jesus of all eternity. You are greater than the angels, and a little less than God. Remember that! It can be invaluable in helping you maintain a proper perspective.

A father was taking his son to the railway station to see him off to college. It was the son's first time to be away from home. All the way to the station the father had been trying to think of the right parting words. They stood together quietly alongside the train. The boarding whistle sounded. The son started to board. The father grabbed his hand, looked him in the eye, and simply said, "Son, remember who you are." That just about took care of everything.

"You are not your own; you were bought with a price" (1 Cor. 6:19, 20), you belong to Christ; you are "His to command"; you are his love-slave (Rom. 6:18, 22). Remember that! It will help to maintain a fixed loyalty.

Christ is within you making you equal to anything that God calls upon you to do. You can do all things through Christ who strengthens you (Phil. 4:13). Remember that always and you will never find yourself excusing yourself from doing his will with the argument that it is beyond your ability.

12. *Look your best always. The gospel takes enough hard knocks without your poor appearance adding to it.*

Since others cannot see the inward change that has taken place in our lives as a result of our new birth, external appearances play an important part of our witness. If we have received internal cleansing and new life there certainly ought to be some external expression of it. This is not to imply that becoming a Christian necessitates acquiring a new wardrobe. It is simply saying that a clean, neat appearance can aid in communicating to others what Christ has done in our lives.

16 Sensing What Is Vital

How does the concerned Christian determine what is highest and best? How does he come to sense what is vital to his life and service in the kingdom? It is all too easy to become occupied with what is important, but with what is not of the greatest of importance. Paul must have realized how easily this can happen for he wrote, "I pray . . . that your love may [display itself in] greater depth of acquaintance and sense what is vital, and approve and prize what is excellent and of real value – recognizing the highest and the best, and distinguishing the moral differences . . . ." (Phil. 1:9, 10, *ANT*).

WHAT IS VITAL?

The big question confronting us is, "How do we determine what is vital in our living as Christians?" When so many interests can capture our attention and so many demands can press us for time, how do we go about determining our priorities? We may often find ourselves lacking in the ability to make such determinations. There may come times when we will sense a need to have God answer Paul's prayer for us – that we "learn to sense what is vital," and "recognize the highest and the best."

Let's turn to God's Word and let him tell us what he thinks is vital to our living as Christians. He doesn't hesitate to point out that there are some things that he considers to be of prime importance that should take precedence over others. Let us consider twelve things that he declares to be of great importance.

TWELVE VITAL THINGS

1. *What is most vital?*

At the hub of all that is vital is the need to know both the Father and the Son. At the threshold of all spiritual life and experience is our coming to know God as he has revealed himself through Jesus Christ. In Jesus' great high priestly intercession for his disciples of all ages, he prayed first of all "that they may know you, the only true God, and Jesus Christ, whom you have sent" (John 17:3).

2. *What is vital in our message?*

Though he had received an "abundance of revelations" directly from the Lord, Paul nevertheless wrote to the Corinthians that the most important thing he had to communicate was the gospel concerning Jesus Christ. He wrote, "For I determined not to know anything among you, except Jesus Christ, and him crucified" (1 Cor. 2:2). Again he wrote, "For I delivered to you as of first importance what I also received, that Christ died for our sins in accordance with the Scriptures, that he was buried, that he was raised on the third day in accordance with the Scriptures" (1 Cor. 15:3, 4).

3. *What is vital in our character?*

Christian character is composed of many fine qualities, any one of which is important. But what is most important? If the disciples of Jesus would be characterized by just one character trait, what would it be? Jesus says, "Love." Love tops the list of aggregate fruit that the Holy Spirit would produce in a life (Gal. 5:22, 23). Heading the list of the qualities that Paul wrote the Colossians to develop was: "And above all these put on love" (3:14). Peter declared love to be the prime consideration: "Above all hold unfailing your love for one another . . . ." (1 Pet. 4:8).

4. *What is vital in our devotion?*

On one occasion Jesus was asked what was the most important thing God required of man: His answer was absolute devotion to God: "The first is, 'Hear, O Israel: the Lord our God, the Lord is one; and you shall love the Lord you God with all your heart, and with all your soul, and with all your mind, and with all your strength'" (Mark 12:29, 30).

5. *What is vital in our worship?*

The word "worship" is never employed in the New Testament to refer to what the church did when it assembled. The term has a much broader meaning. It includes the whole of life lived out in sacrificial service to God. Romans 12:1 captures the idea beautifully: "Present your bodies as a living sacrifice, holy and acceptable to God, which is your spiritual worship." The translators are divided over their rendering of the last word in this passage. Some translate it "worship," and some "serve." It is the Greek word *latreian* and is Paul's favorite word for public worship. In the Revised Standard Version it appears twenty-one times, and is translated "worship" eleven, and "serve" ten. It is the New Testament word for the church's worship, a worship that included all service rendered to God.

6. *What is vital in our services?*

Paul wrote to the Corinthians saying that whether we live in heaven or on earth we should "make it our aim to please" God (2 Cor. 5:9).

How can we please him in our service? By bearing "much fruit" and so proving our discipleship (John 15:8). What is the greatest fruit we can bear? It is the reproduction of ourselves spiritually. In laying out the work for his disciples just prior to his ascension, Jesus said, "Go therefore and make disciples . . ." (Matt. 28:19). Surely these final words of instruction point out what is vital in our service above all other considerations.

7. *What is vital in our aspirations?*

Pursue the kingdom above all considerations! Jesus said, "Seek first his kingdom and his righteousness . . ." (Matt. 6:33). He supported this in his parables of the kingdom. In the parable of the treasure hidden in the field (representative of the kingdom), he has the discoverer sell all that he has and buy that field. In the parable of the pearl of great value (representing the kingdom), he has the merchant sell all that he has and buy that one pearl. The message of the two parables is unmistakable: possession of the kingdom is worth the sacrifice of everything else.

8. *What is vital in our giving?*

Is it that we should tithe or follow some systematic plan of generous giving? In his commendation of the Macedonians for their great generosity, Paul states the reason for it and at the same time sets forth what is vital in our giving: "But first they gave themselves to the Lord and to us by the will of God" (2 Cor. 8:5). And because they did, they therefore "gave according to their means . . . and beyond means, of their own free will" (8:3).

9. *What is the highest and best gift I should seek from God?*

Strange, isn't it, that even some in New Testament times were advocating that the least of God's gifts should be sought after most. So Paul wrote in an attempt to lift their aspirations. Twice listing God's gifts, he exhorted his readers to desire earnestly the higher gifts (1 Cor. 12:8-10, 27-31). He identified and described the highest gift as love (1 Cor. 13), and called upon them to make it their aim (1 Cor. 14:1).

10. *What is vital in my family life?*

Much is said in the New Testament about family life. There seems to be a vital word for each of the four basic relationships that exist in the home, namely: husband-wife, wife-husband, child-parent, parent-child. The wife is to be subject to her husband, as to the Lord; the husband should love his wife as Christ loved the church; the children are to obey their parents in the Lord; and parents are to bring their children up in the discipline and instruction of the Lord (Eph. 5:21-6:4).

11. *What is vital in our warfare?*

First of all, it is vital that we know who the enemy is. So often we are arrayed in battle against those who, in reality, ought to be our allies. Thus we aid the real adversary. The true enemy is that "unholy trinity" – the world, the flesh, and the devil. This alliance of evil forces from both within and without represents the evil spirit world, ungodly mankind, and our own "desires of body and mind" (compare Eph. 2:1-3). These enemies are bent on destroying us and condemning us in hell. It is vital that we set up our defense against these enemies of the soul. Our basic defense against this threefold alliance is our faith (1 Pet. 5:8, 9), the Word of God (compare Eph. 6:17; Matt. 4:1-11), and the support of the Holy Spirit (Rom. 8:13; Gal. 5:16). It is vital that we utilize every resource that God has made available to us to stand against such enemies. We must never rely upon our own ingenuity and power (Eph. 6:10).

12. *What is vital to the church's life?*

Two things are vital to the church's life: (1) the continual introduction of new life into its fellowship, and (2) its own upbuilding. These were the two things highlighted in Jesus' final, parting words to his disciples: "Go therefore and make disciples . . . teaching them to observe all that I have commanded you . . ." (Matt. 28:19, 20). The church must have new life to perpetuate itself, and that new life must be developed and harnessed to perform its ministries.

17 Keep Yourselves From Idols

You probably think that because you have surrendered your life to Jesus that you are now committed solely to him and are completely finished with worshiping other would-be gods. So if someone were to suggest that you might still be serving some idol while at the same time you were serving the Lord Jesus, you might get a bit upset. For after all, you might argue, "When I surrendered my life to Jesus as Lord that put an end to all claims upon my life and loyalty except his alone. It is unthinkable that I would even consider worshiping or serving anyone or anything except him."

You may honestly think that this is so, and it may be, but in view of the fact that you live in a society that is permeated with all kinds of idolatries, it is doubtful that you have escaped their having had some influence upon you. If even the most mature Christians of the first century had such a serious problem contending against idolatry that they had to be warned repeatedly to "Keep yourselves from idols" (1 John 5:21), then there is a strong possibility that there may be some idolatries hidden away in your life that need to be uncovered. Let's consider the possibility.

DID CONVERSION ELIMINATE IDOLATRY?

When the Apostles first began to talk about Christian conversion, they described it as a turning "to God from idolatry, to serve a living and true God" (1 Thess. 1:9). But do not be quick to conclude that conversion put an end to all idolatry in the lives of first century Christians. This becomes clear when you consider two striking exhortations to shun idolatry. They enable us to see that idolatry was a continuing problem for Christians even after they surrendered to Christ. These two passages are striking not only in what they say, but to whom they are said. They are both addressed to Christians.

To the church at Corinth, Paul wrote, "Therefore, my beloved, shun the worship of idols" (1 Cor. 10:14). You would expect Paul to write something like that to the church at Corinth, for it was a congregation carved out of a center of idolatry. And since Corinth was plagued with almost every other major problem imaginable, why be surprised that idolatry was included. You can see how widespread the problem was when you read the Apostle John writing the same thing to the church at large many years later when in his final exhortation in 1 John he wrote, "Little children, keep yourselves from idols" (1 John 5:21). You would have expected that with the passing of time, allowing for considerable growth and maturity to take place, that the first century church would have reached a state of maturity where idolatry would no longer have to be considered as one of her problems. But it was still an issue at the close of the century and, rather than avoid it, the Apostle John honestly faced it and spoke out against it.

The twin sins of idolatry and adultery have plagued the people of God in every age. They have posed more of a problem than any of the other sins and, consequently, God has had to speak out against them more than to the others.

A SYNCRETISM OF THE GODS

It is not so much that the people of God have had a history of completely abandoning God in favor of some idol; it has been more of a syncretism – God and the idol-gods. From Joshua to Malachi the Bible is filled with references to Israel adding to their worship of Jehovah the worship of the gods of the people around them.

Throughout Kings, Chronicles, and the prophets, where reference is made to the "groves," the "high places," and "under the green trees" idolatry is what is being spoken of. You can see the synthesis of God and idols in the worship life of Solomon who was representative of the people of God in his day. Read about him in 1 Kings 11:5-7: "Solomon followed Ashtoreth the goddess of the Sidonians, and Molech the detestable god of the Ammonites. So Solomon did evil in the eyes of the Lord; he did not follow the Lord completely, as David his father had done."

This is not suggest that believers of New Testament times, or of today, would abandon the worship of the God revealed through Christ, but rather that they may add to their worship of God the worship of some other god or gods. Nor does it suggest that anyone today is literally bowing to an idol as such. Our idolatry is more sophisticated. Well, then, what are modern gods? Before we can determine what they are, we must first decide what a god is.

A person's god can be considered to be whatever or whoever comes first in their life and reckoning. It is that force or individual that challenges the right of God within us. It is that which, in the final analysis, determines our choices and claims our time, strength, and consciences. Our god, then can be health, wealth, position, popularity, praise, glory, self – or hopefully it can be "the God and Father of our Lord Jesus Christ," the only true God.

A person's god can be determined by what he worships. The word "worship" is a contraction of the old English "worth-ship" which indicates that our true worship is determined by what we give the worth of our lives to. You can offer some devotion to God by regularly participating in the worship and service of the church and at the same time give the real worth of your life to your business or to some hobby or pleasure.

It takes a keen and honest mind to ferret out and admit the identity of our main object of worship. What are some of the gods that have captured the devotion of modern Christians?

THE IDOL – SELF

The idol which can, with all probability, number the most devotees is *self*. No idol-god has ever been more securely entrenched in the human heart as this one.

The enthronement of self may start at a very early age when the babe in arms is allowed to become a tyrant. Lack of parental discipline in the early years can help develop it in strength. The pleasure of dominating a group on the playground may encourage it yet more. Parents giving in to adolescent pleas, arguing, and tantrums help lift it to the throne. And all unrestricted and uncontrolled growth of the ego serve to help crown it as lord of life.

Once enthroned, this god is almost impossible to dethrone. It took the act of Calvary's cross to break its hold upon the human race. Patient school teachers may try to root it out in the classroom. Athletic coaches may seek to subdue it by an appeal to loyalty to the team. Club leaders and scout masters may shame it into less haughty exposure, but it is a very stubborn idol.

The foundation of this idol is self will, inordinate self-love, self-trust, and self-exaltation. And upon this foundation is reared a superstructure which is one huge capital "I."

The idol "self" is a tyrant god, and an absolute dictator. It demands to be first and central. It always knows what is right and best. It dominates conversations and won't listen to others. It makes choices and decisions in favor of its own interests and desires. Its devotees are selfish, prideful, and conceited. They are self-indulgent, self-seeking, self-pitying, self-defensive, self-conscious, self-righteous, and self-glorifying.

Oh, yes! You can claim Jesus as Lord and yet serve the idol self as a greater god. You can be very active in church, speak a spiritual language, and even teach a Sunday School class, and yet be more devoted to self that you are to Jesus.

"Keep yourselves from idols." Keep yourself from this idol. It is a tyrant that will destroy you.

THE IDOL – "THE CROWD"

Another powerful god of the day is the "crowd" or what E. Stanley Jones used to call "the herd." The creed of this idol is "conform, conform!" Its highest law is "everybody does it." This god will tell you what to say and how to say it, what to eat, what to drink, how to dress, where to go, and what to be.

This god, too, enthrones itself early in life. It capitalizes on what Dr. Harry Overstreet says is the human personality's first need: "the need to belong."

Consider what a hold this idol-god has upon young people. It dictates how they should groom themselves; how they should attire themselves; what their attitude should be toward parents, school, and authorities; what they should pursue for recreation; what kind of music they should listen to – just to list a few things. And so, generally speaking, there are few "individuals" among the youth of our day – they all seem to be carbon copies of some phantom original.

But lest that seems to be hard on young people, take a look at their parents. They too are following the dictates of the crowd. The crowd is dictating their goals and aims in life. It is telling them what they should spend their money for, how they should attire themselves, what kind of homes they should have, what kind of cars they should drive, and on and on. Most people in and out of the church are lost in the crowd! They are an echo instead of a voice. To meet an "individual" is as refreshing as a breath of fresh air.

Are you getting your signals in life from God or from the crowd? Are you paying lip service to Jesus but worshiping the crowd? Are you worshiping God for an hour or so on Sunday and following the crowd the rest of the week?

Lest we think of this god only in terms of the secular world about us, let us be reminded by C. S. Lewis that it can be very entrenched in the church in what Lewis calls the "in crowd." The "in crowd" is composed of those special cliques, groups, and organizations within the church to which we sometimes give our absolute loyalty and devotion. We want to be included by them and have their acceptance and approval more than anything else in life. Whatever the terms for admission or the demands for membership, we will pay the price.

"Keep yourselves from idols." Keep yourselves from this idol.

THE IDOL — PLEASURE

Another great god of today's pantheon is the idol of *pleasure* and *ease.* This isn't a new idolatry. It has been a problem with the people of God in most ages. It seems to revive whenever there is economic prosperity. It was the big problem in both Judah and Israel in the days when Amos the prophet was called to be the spokesman of God. Amos cried out against both nations:

> Woe to those who are at ease in Zion, and to those who feel secure on the mountain of Samaria . . . Woe to those who lie upon beds of ivory, and stretch themselves upon their couches, and eat lamb from the flock, and calves from the midst of the stall; who sing idle songs to the sound of the harp, and like David invent for themselves instruments of music; who drink wine in bowls, and anoint themselves with the finest oils, but are not grieved over the ruin of Joseph! (Amos 6:1, 4-6).

How appropriate the words of Amos would be if he were speaking to today's generation! He might say something like:

> Woe to those who are living in luxury and ease in America and to those who feel secure in their economic prosperity on the continent of Europe. Woe to those who lie upon custom-made brass beds and who are feasting sumptuously on steaks and chops; who lie around singing idle songs to the sound of the guitar or the CD and are inventing for themselves maddening music which stirs one to a craze; who consume beer by the six-pack and liquor by

> the fifth; and who spend billions on fine lotions, shampoos, hair preparations, fragrances, and deodorants, with no concern that over half the world is living on starvation rations.

The creed of this idolatry is: "Pleasure and ease are first considerations, and life must be organized in order to get the maximum of these two things. The motto, "Eat, drink and be merry," has been unchanged down through the ages.

This god would convince you to live solely for weekends, holidays, vacations, and an early retirement to shuffleboard and bingo in which the rest of life would be lived out in idleness and boredom.

The billions in money that this god can extract from his devotees would make God's "tithe" seem like a pittance.

How much time does today's average Christian give in devotion to this god? How would it compare to the time they give to the worship and service of Christ? Would such a comparison indicate the existence of an additional deity in your life?

Don't misunderstand. It's not idolatrous to experience pleasure and enjoy rest and ease. God gave us a capacity for these things. The very thought of God suggests pleasure: "You will fill me with joy in your presence, with eternal pleasures at your right hand" (Ps. 16:11). Pleasure and ease become idolatrous when they are placed above and before God in our affections and devotions.

This idolatry usually creeps into the lives of those who are cold toward Christ or have failed to discover his all-sufficiency. If Jesus isn't satisfying the hungering and longing of the heart, something must, and will. And so satisfaction will be sought by turning to this idolatry.

"Keep yourselves from idols." Keep yourself from this idol. It will lead to disillusionment, disappointment, and in the end destruction.

THE IDOL – MATERIALISM

Twin deity to the god of pleasure and ease is the god of *materialism*. This idol proclaims that "life consists in the abundance of things." Of all the idol-gods, this one has the most extensive propaganda machine. Its advertisement on television, radio, billboards, in newspapers and magazines, plus its materialistic overtures presented in a thousand other ways, seek to brainwash the Christian into accepting its dogma. Its persuasive argument is that what is necessary to really live is to surround yourself with the latest in modern gadgetries and paraphernalia, discover the right cologne, purchase the right car, and get yourself wall-to-wall everything!

This god, who plies the inordinate and almost uncontrollable craving to get and possess, is an idol of unlimited desire. Its claims are impossible to satisfy. The acquisition of one thing can only lead to desire for the next, in an unending pursuit of things.

This god would have you measure all success and achievement in terms of possessions. "What kind of a car do you drive? How big a house do you own – where is it located, how is it furnished?" "How big is your wardrobe – of what quality are your clothes?"

Material things cannot be ignored and ought not to be despised, for after all, God made them and they are ours to be enjoyed. But to a saint things should always be his servant and not his god. Things are meant to serve man, not man things. Life consists of more than possessions.

For Christians to embrace this idolatry indicates a basic dissatisfaction with Christ. It says in effect, "Jesus doesn't really satisfy! I must have something in addition! Jesus is not my 'all in all.' I cannot 'rejoice in the Lord' alone."

"Keep yourselves from idols." Keep yourself from this idol. It is a god with an insatiable appetite. Beware of the covetousness of things!"

THE IDOL – SEX

If anyone should think that Diana, Aphrodite, and Venus are goddesses buried in the past – think again. Because if they were, they have been resurrected and are as much alive today as ever. Western society has become obsessed with sex. It has been exalted to one of the prime positions in the pantheon. It is not only the subject with which books, magazines, movies, and television are preoccupied; it is an emphasis no matter where you turn. For example, automobile manufacturers often try to sell their brand of automobiles with T.V. commercials that picture a voluptuous looking female slithering out from underneath the steering wheel of the product to stand in front of it where she then strips to a scanty bathing suit and then runs toward the surf. Now that may capture the attention of the male audience, but with what information does it provide a prospective car buyer to aid them in deciding whether or not this is the mechanical machine to purchase to provide them with the transportation they need?

In many urban and suburban communities in America it is estimated that 60 to 85% of all high school, college and career young people are engaged in sexual promiscuity with no resulting sense of immorality about it. "It is immoral," they say, "only if you are unfaithful to the one you really love." One is immoral only if they sleep around. These young people define virgin as "an ugly third grader."

Add to this youth scene the high rate of divorce and remarriage, adultery, wife swapping, and fornication in the adult world and you have some idea of how the idol of sex is venerated in our day.

Those who refuse to believe that this obsession with sex is not spilling over into the church are either naive or out of touch with what's going on in today's church. Those who are doing any counseling at all will tell you that the majority of people in the church seeking counsel are seeking it in an attempt to get help in solving problems centering in or relating to sex. Many church leaders have been confronted with the problem of sex sins in the lives of the members of their congregations so often they are beyond being shocked anymore by what anyone reports or confesses.

"Keep yourselves from idols." Keep yourself from the goddess of sex. Since the sex drive is rated number two in the list of human drives, never conclude that you are beyond being seduced by this idolatry. "So, if you think you are standing firm, be careful that you don't fall!" (1 Cor. 10:12).

OVERCOMING IDOLATRY

How can we as Christians live in an idolatrous society and not get caught up in its idolatries? We must first understand that to become a Christian means that we must turn "to God from idols to serve the living and true God" (1 Thess. 1:9). Maybe you didn't know this when you made your decision for Christ. Maybe you weren't even aware that you had any idolatries in your life. If you have now become aware that you have, then denounce them, forsake them, remove from your life any representation or reminder of them, and commit yourself wholeheartedly to Christ as Lord.

If we are to continually keep ourselves from the idols of this world as the Apostle John calls for us to in 1 John 5:21, we need to honestly acknowledge that idolatry is an ever present danger which must be guarded against. Christians live in a society which is obsessed with pleasure, materialism, and sex, and where believers are continually being pressured to conform to ungodly standards and practices. This world will compel all serious disciples to draw upon every resource God has made available to them to enable them to stand in unadultered faith. And they will need to continually stay focused upon Jesus so that his powerful presence in their lives will enable them to repel any possible intrusion of idolatry into their thinking and living.

And also, since an idol can be anything to which we give the worth of our lives and allow to take the place of God whether it be money, career, pleasure, marriage, or whatever, we need to be constantly on guard against the possibility of creating our own idols and worshiping them instead of God. "Keep yourselves from idols."

18 Salvation From Worldliness

Rightly understood *worldliness* is one of the biggest problems the Christian faces. Unfortunately, since many harbor misconceptions about what worldliness is, they fail to see it as a threat to spiritual life and development. They dismiss the subject as being irrelevant to their situation.

Many believers, having read such passages as 1 John 2:16, which describes worldliness, have come up with erroneous ideas about the lust and the pride it condemns. Others have formed their own opinions on the basis of what has been advocated by ultraconservative Christian teachers. They have concluded that worldliness is equated with what one *does*. Sometimes fingers have been pointed at a weak or immature brother or sister and it has been said of them, "He is worldly! He smokes!" Or, "She's worldly; she colors her face up like a Hollywood movie queen." Or, "Look at her short dress; she's worldly!" Or, "Have you noticed the company they've been keeping lately? You can sure see that they're getting worldly!" Or, "Have you heard? They go to movies; they even attend the R-rated ones. How worldly can you get?"

In all this, worldliness is equated with what one *does*. And so long as it is limited to this, it will leave many church members feeling exempt from worldliness on the ground that they don't do such things. Now a worldly person certainly may smoke, wear suggestive clothing, associate with questionable people, and attend sensual movies; but this is not the criterion by which God considers them worldly.

WORLDLINESS DEFINED

To be worldly is to be like the world; "world-like." But what is the world? What is the world like?

When the Bible speaks of the "world" in the context of this discussion, it is certainly not referring to the physical world of God's creating. There is nothing evil about the physical world. God created it all and afterwards said that it was "good." No, when the Bible speaks of the world in the context of this discussion it is not speaking of the beauty of Yosemite National Park or the glory of the Grand Canyon or the vastness of the Sahara Desert.

When the Bible speaks of the world as being evil, it is speaking of the world of men. It is speaking of mankind without God – godless humanity. And what characterizes godless humanity? Three things! And you don't have to be a Bible student to conclude what the three are. You can read about the daily happenings of man in the local newspaper and come to the same conclusion that the Bible does; man is obsessed with *sex*, *things*, and *self*. And his whole philosophy of life centers in acquiring or developing these.

First John 2:16 puts it this way, as translated in *The Paraphrased Epistles:* "For all these worldly things, these evil desires – the craze for sex, the ambition to buy everything that appeals to you, and the pride that comes from wealth and importance – these are not from God. They are from this evil world itself."

On the basis of what this passage declares you can easily conclude that worldliness consists not so much in what we do, as in our assuming the same attitude of heart and philosophy of life that governs the man of the world. It is to become obsessed with one or more of the same three things that he is obsessed with – sex, things, and self. And it is to spend one's life acquiring and developing these.

Being an inward reality therefore, worldliness cannot be identified simply by what we do. To illustrate: here are two deacons who are generally considered to be among the finest members of the congregation. They seem always ready to serve; they are members of several committees, and each is chairman of at least one. They are known for their generosity, they never miss a service or a church function, and they both aspire to be elders. And yet one of them is a godly man and the other is worldly. They labor from different motives!

The motive behind all the first does is a response in love to God who first loved him and demonstrated his love through what Jesus did for him at the cross. His is a labor of love. But the second man labors from an entirely different motive. He is driven by a desire for recognition, praise, and applause. He covets positions of leadership so that he can command and manipulate his fellows. He aspires to be a "ruling elder," directing people and controlling the affairs of the church. His aspirations are identical with those of the man of the world, except that his sphere of operation is the fellowship of the church.

Can we determine who is the godly and who is the worldly man by observing the outward deportment of the two? It is doubtful. But just so that we do not conclude that a few deacons are the only worldly ones in the church, let us hasten to declare that we are all to some degree worldly. Some are more worldly than others, but we all have that side within us which is still subject to thinking and acting like those of this world. There will probably always be a trace of worldliness in all of our lives until we arrive at that perfection promised us in the next world. The only one who has ever been completely free from worldliness was our Lord Jesus Christ.

WRESTLING WITH THE PROBLEM

The great problem with which we wrestle as Christians, therefore, is the temptation to be worldly. This is certainly the biggest temptation that confronts me. I find myself in constant need to have my motives purified by bringing them before Jesus.

For example, I must honestly evaluate my motive for preaching. Why do I so enjoy preaching? Is it because I am afforded an opportunity to share the Word of God with my brethren and thereby help them grow in the grace and knowledge of the Lord Jesus? Is it because of my love for souls? Is it that his love compels me to preach? Or, is it that I enjoy myself? Could it be that I enjoy the applause and acclaim of men? Is it possible that I enjoy the limelight and glamour of it all?

Why have I assumed positions of leadership both inside and outside of the local congregation? Why have I accepted leadership of this committee and presidency of that group? Why? Is it because, like my Lord Jesus, I want to be the servant of all? Or is my motive one of "pride that comes from importance?"

Very often I find myself coming up short. Regrettably, I have to admit that my motive for doing many things is a worldly one. And I am driven to call upon my Savior to purify my motives and deliver me from my worldliness.

The temptation to be worldly was certainly the big problem confronting our Lord Jesus. Being tempted in all manners as we are he was undoubtedly tempted to adopt the philosophy by which this world operates. Wasn't this, in reality, his temptation in the wilderness? Wasn't he tempted to achieve success in the same way the man of the world does? "Jump off the temple and be sensational!" "Start turning stones into bread and you'll soon have the whole world following you." "Accept the leadership of the kingdoms of this world and you will be known and acclaimed by all." But didn't his victory lie in the fact that he chose a different route? His victory lay in the fact that he opposed this world's standard and followed a different ethic. He exhibited a philosophy foreign to this world. His ways were not our ways and his thoughts were not our thoughts. He was other-worldly.

To compare his way with that of the man of this world is to see how very different he was. To achieve greatness the man of the world says, "Get wealth, power, and position and everyone will acclaim you as great." Jesus said, "Whoever would be great among you must be your servant, and whoever would be first among you must be your slave" (Matt. 20:26, 27). The man of the world says, "If you want to be happy and really have an exhilarating life, get pleasure; accumulate material things." Jesus said that if you want real joy, you will find it in a right relationship with God. And if you want pleasure, there are pleasures forevermore in his presence.

The man of the world says, "Defeat your enemies before they defeat you; kick them, club them, kill them!" Jesus said, "Love your enemies . . . and pray for those who . . . persecute you" (Matt. 5:44). The man of the world says if you want the blessed life, be on the receiving end. Jesus said, "It is more blessed to give than to receive" (Acts 20:35).

You can almost determine the course of action that Jesus would take were he still in the flesh, by first concluding what the man of the world would do under a given circumstance, and then doing the very opposite!

VICTORY OVER THE WORLD

We all were born citizens of this world. We started with the physical and then came to the spiritual (1 Cor. 15:46-49). This world has made a great impression upon us. We have accepted its values, we have learned to think in its thought patterns. We have been schooled to act and react as it does. We are products of our world. And until, and unless, something or someone from another world comes along to change us, we will think and act just as this world does until we die.

The message of Jesus tells us that we have been invaded by another world. Heaven has descended to earth. Heaven has sent its King down to this world and in him there is the possibility of a new way of life. Everyone who opens up his life to this heavenly visitor receives a new philosophy of life and a new standard by which to live. He immediately begins to rise above this world and be different. He begins to become other-worldly, like the world from which his new King has come. You see, there is nothing wrong in being worldly if you are like the right world – the other world, the world from which Jesus came.

Rising above and escaping this condemned world begins by receiving Jesus as the "life-giving spirit" (1 Cor. 15:45). By our faith in him we are "born anew from above" (John 3:3; Gal. 3:27-29). The King from above comes to reside within us to begin his great work of refashioning us into his heavenly image (Acts 2:38, 39). It is as we receive Jesus that we are on our way to victory over the world, for victory over the world begins with faith in him: "For everyone born of God overcomes the world; and this is the victory that overcomes the world, even our faith. Who is he that overcomes the world, but he that believes that Jesus is the Son of God?" (1 John 5:4, 5).

How does Jesus do his work? He begins to renew us at our control center. He begins to renew our mind by instilling within us his new message. Romans 12:2 tells us: "Do not conform any longer to the pattern of this world, but be transformed." How? "By the renewing of your *mind.*" See the same exhortation in Ephesians 4:22, 23: "You were taught, with regard to your former way of life, to put off your old self, which is being corrupted by its deceitful desires; to be made new in the attitude of your minds."

Let's see it just once more in Colossians 3:1, 2, 9, 10, "If then you have been raised with Christ, seek the things that are above, where Christ is, seated at the right hand of God. Set your *minds* on things that are above, not on things that are on earth." (Life depends upon what is in your mind and where your mind is.) "Do not lie to one another, seeing that you have put on the new nature, which is being renewed in knowledge after the image of its creator."

What does knowledge have to do with? The mind! We are made into the image of our God as our minds are renewed in the knowledge of the truth that he imparts to us through his Word. What we have become in our minds as citizens of this world must be replaced with the mind of God. In order to be like Christ we must acquire the mind of Christ. "Let this mind be in you, which was also in Christ Jesus," says Paul (Phil. 2:5).

We will be like Christ to the degree that the mind of Christ has been developed within us. "As a man thinks so is he." If we have very little of the mind of Christ developed within us, we shall be forced to rely upon the mind that we have received from the world.

To have the mind of Christ we must yield our minds to the Holy Spirit, who re-educates them through his Word. We must "let the *word* of Christ dwell in [us] richly" (Col. 3:16). As with all education this will be a gradual process and will depend upon our being taught and in our growing "in grace, and in the knowledge of our Lord and Savior Jesus Christ" (2 Pet. 3:18). And, as truth by truth we receive this new knowledge, we shall be "changed into his likeness from one degree of glory to another" (2 Cor. 3:18).

To acquire the mind of Christ and be changed into his likeness is, therefore, to be made unlike this world and be made like Jesus. In this is our salvation from worldliness.

19 Overcoming the Tempter

To Jesus and his Apostles the devil was an ever present threat which they took very seriously. They realized what an enemy he was to faith and continually sought to forewarn believers about him and his tactics that they might be equipped to stand against his attacks. Paul is forever seeking to alert the church to his schemes. He calls upon the Corinthians to exercise forgiveness toward a sinning brother "in order that Satan might not outwit us. For we are not unaware of his *schemes*" (2 Cor. 2:11, emphasis added).

It is obvious from scripture that God wants his children to be informed about the methodology of the devil. In fact, every believer needs to be made aware of his *tactics*, his *target*, and the means of *triumphing* over his attacks.

THE TACTICS OF THE DEVIL

Since the devil cannot possess the Christian because he cannot inhabit that which belongs to God, he is, therefore, confined to being an external enemy. Limited to working from outside the believer, his tactic has become one of diversion. He works primarily through temptations and deceit.

As the "tempter" he seeks to divert the believer from God by offering alternative "shortcuts" to doing his will. This is precisely the tactic he used on Jesus in the temptation account of Matthew four. He suggested that Jesus utilize God's power to turn stones into bread and satisfy his own hunger. It was a double temptation and both were diversionary to God's will. It was a temptation to selfish use of his power. And since his wilderness experience was one of determining the method of his ministry, it was a temptation to reach men by giving them bread or material things. The suggestion offered a futile method for meeting man's deep-seated need. Jesus obviously recognized this to be the case in his rebuttal, "Man does not live on bread alone, but on every word that comes from the mouth of God."

The devil tempted Jesus a second time with the diversionary tactic of sensationalism: "Throw yourself down from the highest point of the temple to the waiting crowds below. God's angels will safely parachute you into their midst and they will follow you with acclamation." But Jesus knew that a ministry based upon sensationalism was doomed to failure. Today's sensation is tomorrow's commonplace and to retain followers by such a means would require greater miracles daily or lose your following. And, too, a belief based on sensationalism is not really faith; it is doubt looking for proof. Jesus dismissed this temptation to a shortcut misuse of God's power with an appeal to scripture: "Do not put the Lord your God to the test."

The third diversionary tactic that the devil used on Jesus to persuade him to come to terms with the world instead of presenting the uncompromising demands of God was the temptation to compromise with the world; be successful in the world by becoming like it. But Jesus rejected this alternative path to success with a reply from Scripture, "Worship the Lord your God, and serve him only."

As the "father of lies" (John 8:44), the devil's tactic is one of *deceit*. In writing to the Corinthians about the devil's deceitfulness, Paul wrote, "I am afraid that just as Eve was deceived by the serpent's cunning, your minds may somehow be led astray from your sincere and pure devotion to Christ" (2 Cor. 11:3). There are at least five ways that the devil seeks to divert believers through deceit.

1. He deceives them about his very own person. And he does it in two ingenious ways. He either deceives people into believing in his non-existence or he leads them to become so obsessed with him and his demons that they become a substitute for God with greater power than his.

2. He uses half-truths, which is the worst form of lying. The scene in the Garden of Eden presents a classical example of this. Eve was approached by the serpent who inquired about the directions God had given about eating from the trees in the garden. Eve told him that the fruit of all the trees was there for their need except one, and about that one God had said, "you must not touch it, or you will die." The serpent replied with a half-truth, "you will not die." And the truth is, they didn't die physically, at least not right away. But they did die spiritually on that day and in time, that resulted in their physical death. They were seduced by a half-truth. The many cults of our day are a witness to the successful employment of the half-truth. Without it they would not exist.

3. The devil seeks to deceive through imitation. Even while the Apostles were still living he had begun to imitate everything basic to the Christian system. He had produced false Christs (Matt. 24:5, 24), false prophets (Matt. 24:11, 24; Acts 13:6; 1 John 4:1), false Apostles (2 Cor. 11:13; Rev. 2:2), false teachers (2 Pet. 2:1; Acts 20:30), false gospels (Gal. 1:6-9), false doctrines (1 Tim. 4:1), a false church (Rev. 2:9), and false miracles (2 Thess. 2:9, 10). Every one of these abound today and are being successfully used to divert people away from biblical Christianity.

4. The devil deceives by perverting scripture. He knows Scripture and can quote it better than any saint. But he always does so to accomplish his own evil purpose of side-tracking believers from the will of God. In Matthew 4:6, he quoted Psalm 91:11, 12 word for word to Jesus. But his purpose in doing so was to pervert the meaning of the passage. He quoted scripture to Jesus as an argument for his misusing the power of God. Does that sound familiar to anyone?

5. The devil deceives by masquerading "as an angel of light" while "his servants masquerade as servants of righteousness" (2 Cor. 11:14, 15). Too many have acquired their concept of the devil from Dante instead of from God. The devil is not a detestable character with a weird, red face, horns, and a long tail with a spear on the end of it. He appears as "an angel of light." And his servants appear to contend for what is right and good. It is quite conceivable to believe that if he were having his full way in the affairs of men, he would have them all be active members of a church that in every way sought to imitate the church of the Lord Jesus, except that there would never be any mention of sin or of Jesus being the Savior from it. Jesus warned against false prophets saying that they would be wolves "in *sheep's* clothing."

THE TARGET OF THE DEVIL

In 1 Peter 5:8 the devil is pictured as one who "prowls around like a roaring lion looking for someone to devour." Therein is a clue to the *target* of his attacks. Lions are a necessary part of the ecological process. Their function is to weed out the weak and sickly of other flocks of animals and keep them from overpopulating by taking some of their strays and their young. In other words, lions feed on the young, the weak, the stragglers, and the sick of the flocks of other animals. These are the same targets of the devil's attack upon the church, God's flock. The devil attacks new babies in Christ, those who are spiritually weak and sick, and those who stray away from the flock and from the protection of its undershepherds. These are the most vulnerable to his attacks because they are at least able to stand against him. The reason why Paul became so concerned for the newly formed Thessalonian church when he came to Athens was because he knew that its members were babes in Christ who were subject to being the devil's target. He offered this as his reason for sending Timothy to check out their faith. He later wrote explaining this, saying, "When I could stand it no longer, I sent to find out about your faith. I was afraid that in some way the tempter might have tempted you and our efforts might have been useless" (1 Thess. 3:5). Paul was not ignorant of the devil's designs. He knew his tactics and he knew who would be his most likely target.

HOW TO TRIUMPH OVER THE DEVIL

The devil is both cowardly and weak. This can be seen by returning to Peter's caricature of him as a "roaring lion" (Paul also caricatures him as a lion in 2 Tim. 4:17, 18). Lions inhabited the Palestinian region during the days of Peter and Paul, who obviously knew something about them. We need to know something about roaring lions.

For one thing, it is the old, weak lions that do most of the roaring. Unable to effectively hunt anymore due to their age, their function becomes one of roaring to frighten prey in the direction of the younger hunting lions.

After a kill lions roar because they are afraid. They are afraid that the jackals, hyenas, and wild dogs will take their meal from them. So they roar in an attempt to frighten them away.

Being weak and cowardly, the devil will flee if actively resisted. And that is precisely what Peter calls upon the believer to do. "Resist him, standing firm in the faith . . ." (1 Pet. 5:9). Resist him not in a defensive way as though you were a fort under attack. But resist him actively like a soldier advancing to meet the enemy. The word "resist" as used here, and elsewhere in James 4:7 and Ephesians 6:10, where the believer is called upon to "resist the devil," implies active, aggressive opposition or resistance.

But how does one actively oppose the devil when he is warned that the devil is not "flesh and blood" to be trifled with as a mere human being, but is a powerful spiritual force? How?

In Ephesians 6:10-18 God gives the strategy. He says that our strength to meet the devil lies in His power and equipping. His equipment is likened to the armament of a Roman soldier. He directs us to "put on the whole armor of God" and describes what it is in detail. Everything that he describes is for defensive protection except for one item, "the sword of the Spirit which is the Word of God." The sword was the one offensive weapon with which a Roman soldier was equipped. His armament and shield were for his defensive protection. But with the sword he could actively oppose an enemy. God is saying, "With my Word you can actively oppose the devil. You can resist him and put him to flight." And if you want to see a perfect illustration of this being done, take a look again at God's pattern Son, Jesus, meeting the devil in the wilderness. Three times the devil came up against him with a temptation and each time Jesus actively opposed him with the Word of God (Matt. 4:4, 6, 10). He "resisted" the devil with the Word of God and "Then the devil left him, and angels came and attended to him" (Matt. 4:11).

We must actively "resist the devil" with the Word of God "and he will flee from us," at least for the time being. And when he later returns, actively resist him with the Word of God in the same way. That's how we will overcome him.

20 The Believer's Authority Over the Devil

The only thing in all God's universe that does not acknowledge the authority of Christ as Lord of all is man. The angels, the animal world, the vegetable world, the whole physical universe – even the demon world – acknowledge his authority.

The demon world has never questioned the authority of Jesus. It has never denied his right to rule as King. The gospels record a number of instances where he demonstrated authority over the evil host. In Luke 4:33-36 a man with a spirit of an unclean demon confronted Jesus and the demon cried out with a loud voice, "Ah! What have you to do with us, Jesus of Nazareth? Have you come to destroy us? I know who you are, the Holy One of God." Jesus exercised his authority over the demon and cast it out of the man. Those who witnessed it were amazed and said to one another, "What is this word? For with authority and power he commands the unclean spirits and they come out." In Mark 1:34 there is this simple statement: "And (he) cast out many demons; and he would not permit the demons to speak, because they knew him to be the Christ." In Mark chapter five there is the story of Jesus meeting a man who was possessed with a legion of demons. Upon meeting Jesus a loud cry came out of the man, "What have you to do with me, Jesus, Son of the Most High God?" With authority Jesus commanded the demons to come out of the man and cast them into a herd of swine.

In Colossians 2:15 the cross is presented as God's verification of the authority of his Son: "He disarmed the principalities and powers and made a public example of them, triumphing over them in it." After his resurrection from the dead Jesus' absolute authority was established in all three realms: "In heaven and on earth and under the earth" (Phil. 2:9-11). The same truth is presented in Ephesians 1:20-22:

> He (God) raised him (Jesus) from the dead and made him sit at his right hand in the heavenly places, far above all rule and authority and power and dominion, and above every name that is named, not only in this age but also in that which is to come; and he has put all things under his feet and has made him the head over all things for the church.

Did not Jesus say just prior to his ascension, "All authority in heaven and on earth has been given to me?"

THE BELIEVER'S AUTHORITY OVER THE DEVIL

If you continue reading into the second chapter of Ephesians you will find that the authority which was given to Christ now belongs to the believer by virtue of his union with him.

Now in and of ourselves we have no authority over the devil. Hebrews 2:14 tells us that in God's order of creation, angels are on a level above men. The order goes like this: God, Jesus, angels, man, animal, vegetable. The point is this, man has no authority over angels, including the fallen ones – the devil and his demons. If man, therefore, is to have authority over the devil and his angels he must be given an authority that is greater than that which he received at creation. It is extremely important to grasp this because until we realize that we have no personal authority over the devil we will live a life of constant defeat in subjection to his authority. And when we do, it will be because we have not appropriated the authority over Satan that has been given us through our Lord Jesus Christ.

Picking up at Ephesians 1:20-23 let us proceed on to chapter two. It begins with the words "And you." That is to say, Christ has been seated at the right hand of God and has been given all authority, but so has the believer. Go on in your reading to Ephesians 2:4-6: "But God, who is rich in mercy, out of the great love with which he loved us, even when we were dead through our trespasses, made us alive together with Christ (by grace you have been saved), and raised us up with him, and made us *sit with him in the heavenly places in Christ Jesus*" (emphasis added). What is Paul teaching? He is teaching us that when God gave his Son authority over the angelic realm, including Satan and his angels, He gave us that same authority because we are in Christ. He who is in Christ has an authority over Satan that ordinary men do not have. At creation man was placed in a position beneath the angels. But through the new creation in Christ the believer is elevated to a position above the angels and is actually seated with Christ in the heavenly places. The order, therefore, becomes: God, Jesus, Christians, angels, animals, vegetables.

If you have been led to believe that you are helpless before the devil, that you can't resist him, that you can do nothing against him and that when he pulls the strings you must dance, you have been deceived by the world's greatest con artist. You have believed the devil's lie. As a believer you have been joined to Christ and share his authority over the devil. You no longer have to go down in defeat as the result of the devil's every attack.

The authority which Jesus had over the devil is illustrated in Matthew 16 where Peter made the great confession that Jesus was the Christ, the Son of the Living God. Jesus said that he would build his church upon that truth and that the gates of Hades would not be able to prevail against it. He then began to tell about his forthcoming suffering, death, and resurrection. "And Peter took him and began to rebuke him, saying, 'God forbid, Lord! This shall never happen to you.' But he turned and said to Peter, 'Get behind me, Satan! You are a hindrance to me; for you are not on the side of God but of men'" (Matt. 16:22, 23). Did Peter learn anything from this demonstration of Jesus' authority over the devil? He certainly did, and he writes about it in his first letter.

TAKING THE OFFENSIVE AGAINST THE DEVIL

In 1 Peter 5:8, 9 Peter writes: "Your adversary the devil prowls around like a roaring lion, seeking someone to devour. Resist him, firm in your faith . . ." Peter knew that the flock of God would be harassed by the devil and he wanted the flock to know what to do when the devil came around. Should believers run or hide or flee? No! Peter says literally, "stand against" the devil. Take the offensive, go after him! The believer can't outrun the devil or hide from him or elude him. He is called upon to offensively "stand against him." There are some things that the Bible tells us to flee, but the devil is never listed as one of them.

In his wilderness temptation Jesus perfectly illustrated how to stand against the devil. When he met the devil he didn't run or try to hide; he stood against him. The only way to meet the devil is to oppose him actively, steadfast in the faith.

There is no standing against the devil apart from an offensive and there will be no victory over him apart from exercising the authority of Christ.

God has not called us to be his children to live a life of constant defeat at the hand of the devil. He never intended for us to live in cowering fear of Satan as though he were absolutely irresistible and we were utterly helpless so that every time he pursues us, we must fall. God has given his children the same authority over Satan that belongs to Jesus; we need to exercise it! The next time Satan starts dogging your steps, exercise your faith, use your authority. Turn to Satan and say, "Get behind me, Satan! I stand against you on the authority of Christ and by the power of his blood!" "Resist – stand against – the devil and he will flee from you."

Printed in the United States
4658